MARINE FISH LARVAE

Morphology, Ecology, and Relation to Fisheries

MARINE FISH LARVAE

Morphology, Ecology, and Relation to Fisheries

Reuben Lasker, Editor

Publisher
Washington Sea Grant Program

Distributor
University of Washington Press
Seattle and London

Publication of this book is supported in part by grant NA81AA-D-00030 from the National Oceanic and Atmospheric Administration to the Washington Sea Grant Program, project E/F-4. The U.S. Government is authorized to produce and distribute reprints for governmental purposes notwithstanding any copyright notation that may appear hereon.

Library of Congress Cataloging in Publication Data
Main entry under title:

Marine fish larvae.

  Includes bibliographies.
    1. Marine fishes—Larvae.   2. Fishes—Larvae.
I. Lasker, Reuben, 1929-
QL639.25.M37   597'.039   81-13073
ISBN 0-295-95883-9   AACR2

College of Ocean and Fisheries Sciences, University of Washington. Printed in the United States of America.

Contents

Fisheries on Coastal Pelagic Schooling Fish   Paul E. Smith   1

Fisheries on Coastal Pelagic Schooling Fish   2

Definitions   2

The Pacific Sardine   4

The Sardine Investigation and CalCOFI   5

Field Studies   6

Sampling to Determine Anchovy Larval Mortality in the Sea   12

Biases   15

Escapement   15

Extrusion   15

Evasion   15

Stage Duration   16

Statistical Transformation   17

Sampling Strategy   18

Larval Transport   18

Critical Period   19

Predation   19

Starvation   20

Preschooling Distribution   20

Spawning Condition   20

Conclusions   21

Larval Anchovy Patchiness   22

Schooling of Adults   22

Statistical Consequences of Larval Patchiness   23

Biological Consequences of Larval Pattern   27

References   29

**Feeding Ecology and Predation of Marine Fish Larvae
John R. Hunter   33**

Feeding Ecology   34

Parental Effects   34

Egg Size, Yolk Quantity, and Starvation   34

Spawning Tactics   36

Swimming Behavior   37

Feeding Behavior   40

Prey Perception and Recognition   40

Motor Patterns   41

Feeding Success   43

Searching Behavior   43

    Prey   44
      Prey Type   44
      Prey Size   45
      Effect of Mouth Size   49
      Nutritive Value of Prey of Different Sizes   51
      Prey Abundance and Density Requirements   55
      Patchiness   58
  Predation   60
    Factors Affecting Vulnerability   60
      Parental Behavior   60
      Starvation   61
      Larval Size and Time of Day   62
      State of Maturity   63
    Types of Predators   64
      Planktonic Invertebrates   64
      Fishes   67
    Conclusions   68
    References   71
The Role of a Stable Ocean in Larval Fish Survival and Subsequent Recruitment   Reuben Lasker   80
    Johan Hjort's Hypothesis of the Larval Fish Critical Period   81
    Does a Good Year Class Depend on a Stable Ocean and Good Food?   82
    Predation on Larval Fishes: An Unknown Factor   84
    Conclusion   85
    References   85
Morphological and Functional Aspects of Marine Fish Larvae H.G. Moser   89
    Acknowledgments   127
    References   127

Figures

Fisheries on Coastal Pelagic Schooling Fish · Smith

Figure 1. The central population of northern anchovy year-class contribution to catch.　7

Figure 2. The arithmetic mean temperature at 30 meters depth for January from 1950 to 1968.　8

Figure 3. The 30-meter temperature anomaly and temperature at the first of four negative anomalies in the contribution to catch, January 1951.　8

Figure 4. The 30-meter temperature anomaly and temperature at the second of four negative anomalies in the contribution to catch, January 1956.　9

Figure 5. The 30-meter temperature anomaly and temperature at the fourth of four negative anomalies in the contribution to catch, January 1975.　10

Figure 6. Estimated abundance of 15 mm standard length anchovy larvae, 1951 to 1975.　11

Figure 7. A comparison of a total life history model of the northern anchovy central subpopulation and sample data from the CalCOFI standard silk net and the California Dept. of Fish and Game midwater trawl.　14

Figure 8. Larval anchovy capture by time of day and size, total California Current area, 1951-1969.　16

Figure 9. Portions of anchovy schools photographed at sea.　28

Feeding Ecology and Predation of Marine Fish Larvae · Hunter

Figure 1. Effect of temperature on swimming speed and feeding rate of northern anchovy fed *Gymnodinium splendens*.　38

Figure 2. Swimming speed of Pacific mackerel, *Scomber japonicus*, larvae and juveniles at 19°, and northern anchovy larvae, *Engraulis mordax*, at 17°C-18°C.　39

Figure 3. Relation between prey size and larval length for 12 species of marine fishes.　46

Figure 4. Relation between width of mouth and ability of *Scomber japonicus* and *Engraulis mordax* to capture prey of various widths.　48

Figure 5. Relation between mouth width and larval length of hake, *Merluccius merluccius*; cod, *Gadus morhua*; Pacific mackerel, *Scomber japonicus*; and three species of anchovy, *Engraulis anchoita*, *E. mordax*, and *E. ringens*.　49

Figure 6. Relation between copepod width and dry weight (excluding naupliar stages).　50

Figure 7. Laboratory growth rates using various foods of *Scomber japonicus* at 22°C, and of *Engraulis mordax* at 16°C.　51

Figure 8. Relation between minimum caloric value of prey required to meet energy needs of larval northern anchovy at 17°C and larval length.　53

Figure 9. Width of foods eaten in the sea by Pacific mackerel larvae of various standard lengths.　54

Figure 10. Change in avoidance ability of four species of clupeoid larvae with length.　63

The Role of a Stable Ocean in Larval Fish Survival and Subsequent Recruitment · Lasker

Figure 1. Fluctuation of the sardine catch around Japan.　81

Morphological and Functional Aspects of Marine Fish Larvae · Moser

Figure 1. Transformation of the European eel, *Anguilla anguilla*, from the leptocephalus to the juvenile.   91

Figure 2. Stations at which plankton collections were made during the Danish eel investigations, 1903-1922, and areal distribution of *Anguilla anguilla* larvae based on plankton surveys.   92

Figure 3. Larvae of clupeiforms: *Engraulis mordax*, *Sardinops sagax*, and *Etrumeus teres*.   95

Figure 4. Larvae of argentinoid smelts showing various eye types: *Bathylagus milleri*, *B. wesethi*, and *B. ochotensis*.   97

Figure 5. Larvae of stomiatoids: *Vinciguerria lucetia*, *Diplophos taenia*, *Ichthyococcus ovatus*, *Danaphos oculatus*, *Maurolicus muelleri*, and *Sternoptyx* sp.   98

Figure 6. Larvae of stomiatoids: *Stomias atriventer*, *Bathophilus nigerrimus*, and melanostomiatid.   99

Figure 7. Various eye shapes of marine teleost larvae: *Bathylagus milleri*, *B. wesethi*, *Myctophum nitidulum*, and *Idiacanthus fasciola*.   100

Figure 8. Theoretical relation of eye stalk length to perception distance in fish larvae.   101

Figure 9. Larvae of demersal myctophiforms: *Synodus lucioceps*, *Chloropthalmus agassizi*, aulopid, and bathysaurid.   102

Figure 10. Larvae of midwater myctophiforms: *Ahliesaurus berryi*, *Evermannella balbo*, *Lestidiops ringens*, and *Scopelarchoides nicholsi*.   103

Figure 11. Larvae of myctophine lanternfishes: *Protomyctophum crockeri*, *Hygophum reinhardti*, *Myctophum aurolaternatum*, *Myctophum asperum*, and *Loweina rara*.   104

Figure 12. Larvae of myctophine lanternfishes: *Diogenichthys lanternatus*, and *Diogenichthys atlanticus*.   106

Figure 13. Larvae of lampanyctine lanternfishes: *Triphoturus nigrescens*, *Diaphus theta*, *Lobianchia dofleini*, *Lampanyctus achirus*, and *Lampanyctus* sp.   107

Figure 14. Larvae of notolychnine and gymnoscopeline lanternfishes: *Notolychnus valdiviae*, *Ceratoscopelus townsendi*, *Lepidophanes gaussi*, *Lampadena urophaos*, *Notoscopelus resplendens*, and *Lampanyctodes hectoris*.   108

Figure 15. Young of gadiforms: *Merluccius productus*, *Bregmaceros macclellandii*, and *Eretmophorus kleinbergi*.   110

Figure 16. Young of gadiforms: *Krohnius filamentosus*, *Carapus acus* and exterilium larva.   111

Figure 17. Larvae of lampridiforms: *Trachipterus* sp. and *Lophotus* sp.   112

Figure 18. Larvae of lampridiforms: *Zu cristatus* and *Regalecus glesne*.   113

Figure 19. Larvae of atheriniforms: *Cypselurus heterurus doderleini*, *Hemirhamphus sajori*, *Tylosurus melanotus*, and *Cololabis saira*.   114

Figure 20. Larvae of acanthopterygii showing well-developed spination: *Anthias gordensis*, *Epinephelus* sp., *Holocentrus vexillarius*, *Antigonia rubescens*, *Dactylopterus volitans*, *Caulolatilus princeps*, *Champsodon snyderi*, *Forcipiger longirostris*, acanthurid, and *Ranzania laevis*.   116

Figure 21. Larvae of scombroids: *Thunnus albacares*, *Gempylus serpens*, *Luvarus imperialis*, *Istiophorus americanus*, and *Xiphias gladius*.   117

Figure 22. Larvae of *Sebastes*: *S. oblongus*, *S. macdonaldi*, *S. jordani*, *S. paucispinis*, *S. levis*, and *S. melanostomus*.   119

Figure 23. Larvae of scorpaenids: *Helicolenus dactylopterus*, *Scorpaena guttata*, *Scorpaenodes xyris*, *Pontinus* sp., *Sebastolobus altivelis*, and *Ectreposebastes imus*.   121

Figure 24. Larvae of pleuronectid flatfishes: *Glyptocephalus zachirus*, *Microstomus pacificus*, *Pleuronichthys decurrens*, and *P. ritteri*.   122

Figure 25. Larvae of bothid flatfishes: *Bothus constellatus*, *Taeniopsetta ocellata*, *Laeops kitaharae*, and *Arnoglossus japonicus*.   123

Figure 26. Larvae of paralichthyid, cynoglossid and soleid flatfishes: *Citharichthys platophrys*, *Paralichthys californicus*, *Syacium ovale*, *Symphurus atricauda*, and *Achirus lineatus*.   124

Figure 27. Larvae of lophiiforms and *Schindleria*: *Lophius piscatorius*, *Histrio histrio*, *Caulophryne jordani*, *Cryptosaras couesi*, *Edriolychnus schmidti*, and *Schindleria praematurus*.   126

Tables

Fisheries on Coastal Pelagic Schooling Fish · Smith

Table 1. Example of negative binomial weighted model solution for 14 size groups of anchovy larvae.   13

Table 2. Anchovy school diameter frequency distribution by school and biomass.   24

Table 3. Selected parameters of northern anchovy schools in California coastal waters.   25

Table 4. Sample frequency distribution of Pacific sardine eggs and larvae.   26

Feeding Ecology and Predation of Marine Fish Larvae · Hunter

Table 1. Vulnerability to starvation of eight marine fish larvae at the time of first feeding.   35

Table 2. Average densities of microcopepods in the sea.   55

Table 3. Food density thresholds for six species of marine fish larvae.   56

Table 4. Most abundant large planktonic invertebrate predators taken in standard oblique plankton hauls along the California coast in 1954, 1956, and 1958 and their occurrence with larval anchovy.   66

Foreword

Under the Washington Sea Grant Program funds have been available since 1971 which enabled the College of Fisheries to invite leading investigators in the field of management and conservation of aquatic natural resources and the biology of important exploited species to deliver lecture series on timely topics. Six of these have subsequently appeared in printed form and serve as up-to-date accounts for use by fisheries students and investigators.

In 1979 appeared the first of a two-part account of the topic of early life history of marine fishes dealing with the egg stage, by Dr. G. Hempel. The present volume and second part discusses the larval stage. Originally Dr. Reuben Lasker, Chief of the Coastal Fisheries Resources Division, Southwest Fisheries Center, National Marine Fisheries Service, was approached and agreed to deliver alone the entire lecture series. However, due to unforeseen circumstances he had to renege on this promise. Rather than cancelling the lectures Dr. Lasker drew upon the rich supply of innovative and talented investigators at the Southwest Fisheries Center, and Dr. P. E. Smith, Dr. H. G. Moser, and Dr. J. R. Hunter, agreed to share the burden of giving some lectures each on rather short notice. This in itself is a testimony to the breadth and depth a study on marine fish larvae occupies at this center and to which Dr. Lasker has been a contributor and constant source of inspiration over a quarter of a century.

His bubbling enthusiasm for the subject matter, the larval stage of pelagic marine teleosts and its associated mortalities as a main factor in shaping the numerical strength of a year class, brought him back to the ongoing lecture series at the earliest opportunity, and Dr. Lasker presented an overview to set the stage for the other contributions. In the end he edited all papers in this volume which represents the most authoritative account of the larval life history of marine fishes. One additional topic was added to the series by Dr. A. W. Kendall of the Northwest Center of the National Marine Fisheries Service on Early Life History of Eastern North Pacific Fishes in Relation to Fisheries Investigations. Because of the somewhat different subject matter, this lecture has been published separately as Washington Sea Grant Technical Report WSG 81-3.

Ole A. Mathisen

20 July 1981

Fisheries on Coastal Pelagic Schooling Fish

Paul E. Smith

Fisheries on Coastal Pelagic Schooling Fish

Fishery science is undergoing a transition from the management of "stocks" of fish to the management of the entire fish component of an "ecosystem." The major barriers in this transition in the pelagic biosphere are not the construction of theoretical models but are likely to be the logistical problems of assembling verification of theory from field observations.

The nature of the transition from fish stock management to management of the fishery elements in an ecosystem is in part apparent from the broadly-based studies of the California Cooperative Oceanic Fisheries Investigations (CalCOFI). Following the 1947 collapse of the northern "stock" of the Pacific sardine, then the largest fishery of the United States, the CalCOFI program was instigated and funded by the fishermen and organized by Dr. Frances Clark, director of marine research for the California Dept. of Fish and Game, Dr. O. Elton Sette of the U.S. Bureau of Commercial Fisheries, and Prof. Harold U. Sverdrup, director of the University of California Scripps Institution of Oceanography. Their broad mandate was to determine the causes of the major fluctuations of production of fish stocks in the California current region.

From the CalCOFI research program it is apparent that multispecies fishery management in the context of an ecosystem will require several intermediate steps from our current skills at stock management. To emphasize the massive scope of such a transition, the survival of a year-class of fish like anchovy or sardine off California may depend on food strata less than a meter thick; at the same time these fish may be preyed upon appreciably (Smith, 1978a) by young albacore spawned 10,000 kilometers away in the western tropical Pacific or by northern fur seal females born 10,000 kilometers away in the Bering Sea.

Definitions

(1) Stock—that portion of a fish subpopulation available to a fishery. This could be the entire subpopulation.

(2) Subpopulation—that portion of a population which is likely to be interbreeding.

(3) Population—that portion of a species which is alive at a particular time.

(4) Species—a group of organisms continuous in time which was likely to be capable of interbreeding.

(5) Guild—a group of populations dependent on the same set of populations for food.

(6) Ecological community—a group of populations likely to be found together.

(7) Ecosystem—a community of organisms and their environment.

The most critical stage of the transition from stock management to ecosystem management from a fisheries standpoint is the guild. In the California Current system and several other productive areas of temperate and tropical seas, the guild of schooling pelagic organisms is an obvious repetitive feature. The major populations of schooling pelagic organisms in the California Current are the northern anchovy, *Engraulis mordax*; the Pacific sardine (or pilchard), *Sardinops sagax*; the jack (or horse) mackerel, *Trachurus symmetricus*; the Pacific mackerel, *Scomber japonicus*; the Pacific saury, *Colalabis saira*; the Pacific hake (or whiting), *Merluccius productus*; and the market squid, *Loligo opalescens*. The guild depends to varying degrees on large phytoplankton, zooplankton, and small fish. Most of the same genera occur together off Europe, South Africa, Australia, Japan, and the west and east coasts of South America, and major fisheries concentrate on the schooling pelagic guild. As repetitive as the group of genera is the tendency for the major stocks to collapse under fishery pressure.

The importance of the guild of coastal pelagic schooling organisms is that it is a human protein source perpetually capable of providing several kilograms of fish per year per capita of the world population. These fish are close to land, and their tendency to be schooled and for the schools to be aggregated makes their capture very efficient by concentrated purse seine fleets. This capture efficiency is also a major hazard to the perpetuity of the yield, and recurrent collapses of members of the pelagic schooling guild are the topics of much applied research in each region of the world where these fisheries occur. The inevitable fluctuations in the available stocks may be smoothed at the market place because canned and fish meal products can be stored for extended periods.

Schooling pelagic fish occupy a hydrographic province whose geopraphic extent can double or triple in a few years and return to the original as rapidly. Also, a pelagic schooling fish occupies a very small portion of its available environment at any instant, but it occupies it very intensely. For instance, we have data which suggest that under each square meter of sea surface there may be 15 kilograms of fish within a fish school (Hewitt et al., 1976). The fish schools occupy only 0.5 percent of the area which is physiologically defined for them. The early nomenclature, particularly density-dependent and density-independent, is generally inadequate for describing survival in schooling fish. Where the habitat is geographically circumscribed, stock size dependence and density dependence may be identical, but in an area of flexible hydrographic boundaries, density dependence operates on a local scale, such as on the kilometer scale, and stock size dependence operates on a scale of hundreds of kilometers. This distinction is very important for monitoring a fishery because the fishery normally operates not over the ecological range or the entire hydrographic province on which the fish depend, but only over a small part of the habitat where fish concentrate from time to time and are likely to be encountered by fishing boats.

The Pacific Sardine

What really did happen to the Pacific sardine? Our perception of the situation is necessarily simple, because we lack data necessary to erect a complex hypothesis. However, our perception of what happened to the Pacific sardine was important for determining the research attack taken at the Southwest Fisheries Center and for explaining why we are spending so much time in the area of larval and juvenile studies.

The Pacific sardine once occupied an area from the tropics to Vancouver Island. The virgin population was made up of about ten spawning year classes in addition to the year classes about to recruit, and the older ones of these migrated along the entire west coast of America. There were three stocks. One stock we call the northern subpopulation of the Pacific sardine and it is this one that spawned in the spring, roughly from the upwelling area off Punta Eugenia, Baja California, to San Francisco. Another subpopulation occurred south of Punta Eugenia, and one still occurs in the Gulf of California. The limit to spawning was the 13°C isotherm; Pacific sardine eggs do not survive in water colder than 13°C. Following spawning, it appears that the older fish migrated to the north, somewhat in proportion to their size—the largest fish traveling the furthest—and separated out along the coast to feed in the extremely rich area which terminates the west wind drift of the Northern Pacific Ocean. It is, as well, the primary site of an eastern boundary current upwelling system. There they gained weight for the season and moved back to southern California the following spring to spawn.

The time course of the Pacific sardine fisheries has been assembled by Ahlstrom and Radovich (1970). The Pacific Northwest landed up to 100,000 tons and became the first area to notice the changing migration patterns of the Pacific sardine. The fishery there virtually stopped in 1945 and has not yet recovered. Central California was the primary site for phytoplankton production and the place of the largest fishery, half a million tons. The sardine fishery there had collapsed by the end of 1955, after two population failures. Southern California, the residence of the younger sardines, had a sustained fishery that lasted into the 1960s and then it too was abruptly terminated in

1964. The Baja California fishery caught both the southern and northern stocks; it now catches anchovy while it continues at a low level of sardine fishing. That fleet shifts seasonally into the Gulf of California, where the primary sardine fishery is now conducted.

Murphy (1966) described what happened to the Pacific sardine. The Pacific sardine had ten spawning year classes in the virgin stock. Since short-term anomalies in the environmental conditions are more common than long-term anomalies, the sardine, which has ten spawning year classes, is not very prone to periodic recruitment failures. However, when the sardine population was reduced to a population having only two spawning year classes: two recruitment failures in a row virtually destroyed the stock. Murphy believes that this is the direct effect of fishing because fishing changes the age composition of the stock. This final age composition was then more vulnerable to shorter and shorter term environment anomalies, which eventually destroyed the stock.

I have made a slight addition to the Murphy hypothesis regarding reducing the number of year classes to two. I believe it is also true that anomalies which cover small areas are more common than environmental anomalies which cause year-class failure over a large area. The sardine stock collapsed from north to south. This probably also implies that the sardine occupied a smaller and smaller area of the pelagic environment and, having occupied these smaller areas, was then more subject to anomalies over a small area. The changing year-class structure is the basis of Murphy's main hypothesis on why the Pacific sardine collapsed. Added to this is the probability that a smaller distribution area is more subject to destructive anomalies.

The Sardine Investigation and CalCOFI

CalCOFI is the California Cooperative Oceanic Fisheries Investigations. It was begun by state, federal, and university scientists at the request of the fishermen and processors who were put out of business by the drastic sardine population collapse. The industry wanted to know if population variations could be predicted and if fishery regulations would shield it from these variations.

To find out, they taxed themselves from 1947 to 1978 a dollar a ton on all of the "wetfish" catch to support research on pelagic California commercial fish. The fishermen themselves were interested enough to find the causes for these drastic declines in population. They took a large fraction of their catch dollar and put it toward specific research to study these variations. Even though the actual dollar amount was never very large in terms of a major fishery research program, the program guided and coordinated the research of three major organizations for more than thirty years. So the less than half a million dollars put in by the fishermen out of their own pockets guided the use of four or five times that much research money over this period.

The primary reason the processors and fishermen withdrew their financial support in 1979 was not that they were unhappy with the progress, but that the federal Fishery Conservation Management Act (FCMA) 200-mile-limit legislation had taken the responsibility for the management of these fish, and it was concluded at this time that private industry could now retire from its funding of these activities. Today the primary research components of CalCOFI—the Southwest Fisheries Center of the National Marine Fisheries Service, the California Department of Fish and Game, and the Marine Life Research program of the Scripps Institution of Oceanography—continue their research in the same coordinated fashion but with broader objectives.

Field Studies

The primary activity of CalCOFI has been the field population study. A large proportion of ship time was planned around studying pelagic schooling populations in the field. This was not done at the expense of monitoring the catch in the age, weight, condition, sex ratio—those programs continued. Two additional surveys were mounted. One was a sea survey of juveniles and adults conducted by the California Dept. of Fish and Game. They began by attracting fish to night lights and catching them with lift nets or dynamite. Their techniques for studying sardines had to be modified so that they could also study anchovy, jack mackerel, and Pacific mackerel.

The second major field population survey was conducted on eggs and larvae. In 1949, when high seas oceanographic work started, there was no capability to capture adults on a routine basis over their entire range. One solution was to monitor spawning behavior, stock size, and spawning. Particularly important to the interpretation of field data has been the laboratory study phase which began in the mid-50s.

What do we expect from a larval survey? At the beginning, larval surveys to determine distribution and abundance of eggs and early larvae were supposed to give us an index of the spawning biomass; the later larvae were to be used to project how many survivors there would be from each year's spawn. The precision of larval surveys is greater with small stock sizes than it is with large stock sizes. The catch-per-unit-of-effort monitoring, done when a fishery is operating, is accurate with a large stock size and becomes less dependable with small stocks. The larval survey therefore augments the normal fishery monitoring in a useful way. The spawning surveys also monitor changes in spawning biomass. One obvious shortcoming has been that the best estimates of the abundance of surviving large larvae will not predict in a correlative sense the size of the recruitment.

Ahlstrom (1965) examined the CalCOFI larval surveys, the recruitment of fish into the fishery, and the oceanographic conditions on the spawning grounds. He reasoned that variations in "general productivity" could not have

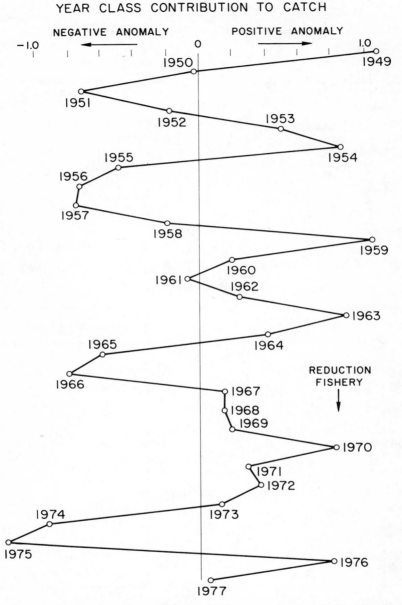

Figure 1. The central population of northern anchovy year-class contribution to catch. The numerical contribution on each year's catch by each year-class is calculated from the sum of the proportionate contribution for the first through fourth years. The sum was normalized for the purpose of constructing a bilaterally symmetric time series with a mean of zero, and the anomalies are expressed in the number of standard deviations. The fisheries before 1966, from which these data were derived, were small and local. The reduction fishery, which began in 1966, has been sampled by the California Dept. of Fish and Game in the Los Angeles area (after Smith et al., in press).

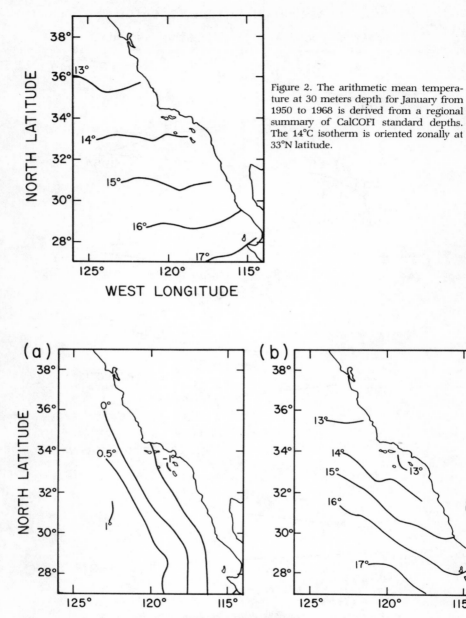

Figure 2. The arithmetic mean temperature at 30 meters depth for January from 1950 to 1968 is derived from a regional summary of CalCOFI standard depths. The 14°C isotherm is oriented zonally at 33°N latitude.

Figure 3. The 30-meter temperature anomaly (a) and temperature (b) at the first of four negative anomalies in the contribution to catch (Fig. 1), January 1951. The 14°C isotherm is oriented diagonally and the 13°C isotherm is in the Southern California Bight. The anomalies are oriented meridionally; and regional anomalies are negative within 100 n.mi. of the coast: part of the Southern California Bight has more than 1°C negative anomaly.

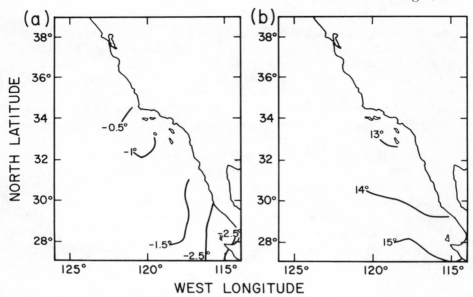

Figure 4. The 30-meter temperature anomaly (a) and temperature (b) at the second of four negative anomalies in the contribution to catch (Fig. 1), January 1956. The 14°C isotherm is at 30°N latitude, 180 miles south of the mean position. The 13°C isotherm encompasses the Southern California Bight, and the anomalies of from 0.5°C to 2°C colder than normal over the entire distribution of the central subpopulation of the northern anchovy.

been a major control on these fish stocks because a general decline should have been observable in all species, but the good years for anchovy, sardine, and Pacific mackerel did not coincide. In fact, he stated, some of the "poorest years for larval survival have been years of high productivity," as measured by high standing crops of sardines. Even with these changes in the success of year classes, he found no significant variation in relative numbers of large larvae and concluded "this consistency pulls the rug out from under any attempts to relate variation in larval survival to environmental conditions." At the time of his study, only eight annual surveys (1951–58) had been analyzed.

Twenty-nine years of age composition data have been assembled from the bait, cannery, and reduction fisheries on the central subpopulation of the northern anchovy (Fig. 1). Large-scale features of the California Current were examined for some of the maxima and minima in anchovy year-class "contribution to catch," a measure of spawning success (Smith and Haight, 1980). One constant feature, a large-scale cold anomaly in the Southern California Bight (Smith et al., in press), coincided with the four episodes (1951, 1955–56–57, 1965–66, and 1974–75) of anomalously low contribution to catch. Moderate and high contribution to catch resulted indiscriminantly from average and warm conditions.

The diagnostic sign of these years of poor contribution of a year-class to catch may be seen from comparing the average January temperature at 30 meters over the distribution of the northern anchovy central subpopulation (Fig. 2) with the same temperatures in January of 1951, 1956, and 1975 (Figs. 3, 4, and 5) and their resultant anomalies. The average plot has the 14°C isotherm parallel to and overlying 33°N latitude. In the "cold" years the 14°C isotherm is no longer parallel to or overlying 33°N latitude. The nearshore end is replaced by 13°C water. An estimate of abundance of the larger larvae (15 mm) similarly shows some concordance with the "poor" recruitment years (Fig. 6).

Not only the abundance but the timing of the peak abundance of large larvae appears important. In the failing years—1951, 1956, 1965, 1966, and 1975—the spring and summer abundances were low. None of the regional average temperatures shown is near the lethal limit for anchovy (Ahlstrom, 1965), so one must conclude that the temperature is an indicator rather than the cause of adverse conditions for survival. Some of the possible causative factors (such as low vertical stability and mixing) will be discussed in the following section.

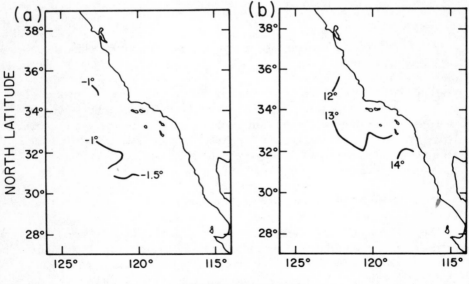

Figure 5. The 30-meter temperature anomaly (a) and temperature (b) at the fourth of four negative anomalies in the contribution to catch (Fig. 1), January 1975. The 14°C isotherm has been replaced by the 13°C isotherm, and the temperature anomaly is from 1°C to 1.5°C below average over the whole distribution of the northern anchovy.

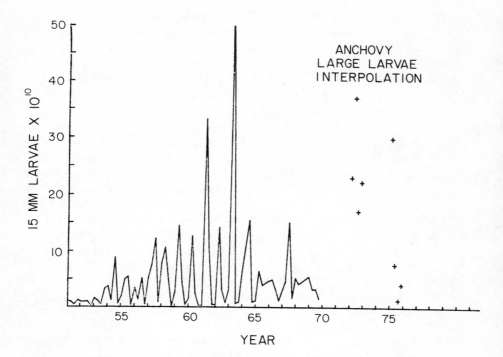

Figure 6. Estimated abundance of 15 mm standard length anchovy larvae, 1951 to 1975. Low relative contribution to catch occurred in four sets—1951, 1955–56, 1965–66, and 1974–75. Moderate and high contribution to catch cannot be distinguished at the 15 mm stage. Values are quarterly estimates which result from single cruises in 1961–65; in other years the quarterly values result from more than one cruise in winter, spring, and summer and usually a single cruise in autumn.

Sampling to Determine Anchovy Larval Mortality in the Sea

It is impossible to make unbiased estimates of the number of fish larvae in the sea, and precise estimates require many carefully taken and sorted samples. The major biases are caused by extrusion through the meshes of nets used to capture embryos and early larvae and evasion of the approaching net by older larvae. The major source of imprecision is the tendency of larvae of all sizes to be aggregated, or "patchy." Larval mortality may be determined from a sufficiently large set of imprecise samples by monitoring the sources of bias. We may begin to specify small-scale sampling requirements for describing larval mortality by examining the mass effects of mortality on a very large set of samples (> 30,000) over the CalCOFI grid area (200,000 sq.n.mi.) for the 24-year period, 1951–1975.

It would be foolhardy to specify sampling requirements in detail without some information on a hypothesis to be tested. For example, a space-extensive survey might be required to test the null hypothesis about larval transport—"no important effects on mortality are due to the area in which they are spawned." A time-intensive survey would be required to test the null hypothesis about critical period—"no discernible differences in mortality occur over short periods." Thus for a widely distributed species like the northern anchovy, a test of the "larval transport" hypothesis would require a different sampling emphasis from a test of the "critical period" hypothesis.

For the purpose of this chapter, then, I will discuss some significant sources of bias and how a sampling program would be established to test several hypotheses relating to larval anchovy survival in the sea. Knowledge of the distribution of mortality in the life cycle, variations in mortality, and models of cause and effect should provide background for rational management of a fishery on this stock by direct monitoring and prediction of recruitment and population size.

Anchovy mortality is extremely high, and each successive life stage represents an improving chance for survival (the "Type IV" survival curve of Slobodkin, 1962). I have arbitrarily divided the life cycle into six stages: embryonic, early larval, late larval, juvenile, prerecruit, and adult. In Table 1, I have listed these stages with nominal durations, estimated daily mortality rates, and the abundance of a hypothetical cohort spawned in a week and evaluated at each of the stage margins. The model has been constructed so that crude estimates of fecundity (Hunter and Goldberg, 1980) allow the population model to represent a stationary population (Fig. 7). The model is

Table 1. Example of negative binomial weighted model solution for 14 size groups of anchovy larvae (Bissell, 1972; Zweifel and Smith, 1980).

Group	Preserved size (mm)	Recorded preserved size (mm)	Average* live size (mm)	Age from spawn (days)	Days in interval	Predicted LCL	Predicted UCL (No. 10m^{-2})	Predicted Mean
1	3.25	2.5	3.23	1.98	1.95	3.1×10^2	4.8×10^2	3.9×10^2
2	3.25–4.25	3.75	4.49	6.45	4.69	1.8×10^2	2.5×10^2	2.1×10^2
3	4.25–5.25	4.75	5.57	9.32	2.67	1.1×10^2	1.5×10^2	1.3×10^2
4	5.25–6.25	5.75	6.62	11.84	2.40	6.8×10^1	9.0×10^1	7.8×10^1
5	6.25–7.25	6.75	7.66	14.14	2.21	4.2×10^1	5.5×10^1	4.8×10^1
6	7.25–8.25	7.75	8.68	16.27	2.07	2.6×10^1	3.4×10^1	3.0×10^1
7	8.25–9.25	8.75	9.68	18.29	1.97	1.6×10^1	2.1×10^1	1.8×10^1
8	9.25–10.25	9.75	10.69	20.22	1.90	1.0×10^1	1.3×10^1	1.2×10^1
9	10.25–11.25	10.75	11.69	22.09	1.85	6.2×10^0	8.3×10^0	7.2×10^0
10	11.25–12.25	11.75	12.68	23.92	1.81	3.8×10^0	5.3×10^0	4.5×10^0
11	12.25–13.25	12.75	13.68	25.71	1.78	2.3×10^0	3.4×10^0	2.8×10^0
12	13.25–14.25	13.75	14.68	27.48	1.76	1.4×10^0	2.2×10^0	1.8×10^0
13	14.25–15.25	14.75	15.67	29.24	1.76	6.7×10^{-1}	1.1×10^0	8.6×10^{-1}
14	15.25–16.25	15.75	16.66	30.97	1.71	5.2×10^{-1}	9.0×10^{-1}	6.9×10^{-1}

* Corrected for abrasion and shrinkage (Theilacker, 1980).
LCL = lower confidence limit.
UCL = upper confidence limit.

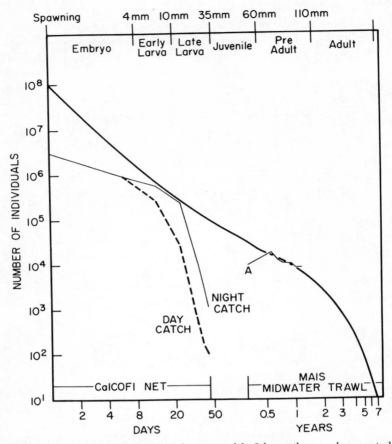

Figure 7. A comparison of a total life history model of the northern anchovy central subpopulation and sample data from the CalCOFI standard silk net (Kramer et al., 1972) and the California Dept. of Fish and Game midwater trawl (Mais, 1974). The main bias at the embyro stage is extrusion through the mesh of the net. The main bias of the early larval stage is daytime evasion of the net, and the main bias of the late larval stage is day and night evasion of the net. Further evidence of nighttime evasion of nets by fish larvae contained in a plankton purse seine compared with a towed plankton net is given by Murphy and Clutter (1972). The point "A" represents occasional juvenile anchovy captured in the midwater trawl liner. These juveniles may be underestimated by behavioral, geographic, and bathymetric differences from the adults.

artificial because absolute mortality rate estimates are available only for the early larvae (Zweifel and Smith, in press) and for the adults (MacCall, 1974). These rates are joined only to satisfy the condition of stationarity. The reader is cautioned that the population of anchovy probably does not exhibit stationarity and that all estimated rates have been assembled from multiyear samples over wide ocean areas.

Biases

Four biases have been evaluated: escapement, extrusion from nets, evasion from nets, and stage duration. The first three are negative biases, but deviation in stage duration can contribute either a positive or a negative bias. The nature of these biases is discussed here in preparation for the next section on sampling procedures and program (tactics and strategy) for the analysis of population change through studies of mortality at sea. Another bias may result from statistical transformation of abundance data.

Escapement

Escapement is defined here as the passage of the sampled organism through the mesh apertures of a net. A major consideration, then, is the size of the mesh aperture. As a first approximation it may be assumed that escapement will occur when the minimum dimension of the anchovy larva is less than the diagonal of the mesh aperture. The selection of an appropriate mesh aperture is important because larger apertures yield variable retention when, for example, filamentous algae impart retention characteristics of smaller nominal mesh apertures. Smaller than necessary net apertures retain more plankton from which the larvae will have to be sorted; costs of sorting anchovy larvae from other plankton are high, so this too is an important consideration.

Extrusion

Extrusion in this context is the forcing of the larvae through the meshes of the net. This can result either from improper design of the net or from towing the net at too high a speed. Towing speed may be acceptable on the average, but an increase in speed near the end of the tow can extrude larvae retained for most of the tow duration. Extrusion may also be increasingly probable with the lengthening of towing time or with vertical towing in rough seas. As a first approximation, extrusion and escapement should be evaluated at tow speeds of 70 cm/sec with increments of 20 cm/sec (Smith and Richardson, 1977, Table 3.2.3).

Evasion

Evasion is the swimming of larvae out of the volume to be filtered by the net. Evasion is demonstrable from day/night (Fig. 8) differences in catch of anchovy larvae and sardine larvae as small as 5 mm preserved length. The existence of a day/night difference also demonstrates night avoidance (Smith and Richardson, 1978). For a first approximation the evasion bias can be regarded as total when the length of the anchovy larva is 3 percent of the radius of the net when the net is being towed at 5 larval body lengths per second. For bridle-free nets (which are recommended), larvae will be sampled somewhat better. Evasion will likely be reduced by improved filtration efficiency and nets with low visual contrast.

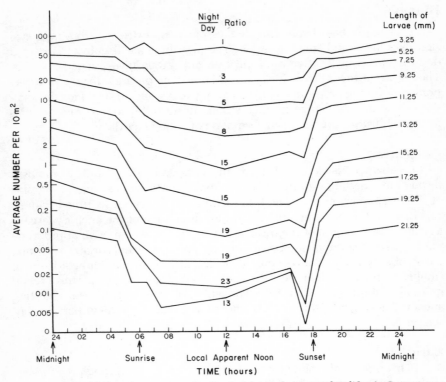

Figure 8. Larval anchovy capture by time of day and size, total California Current Area, 1951–1969. Marked asymmetry at dusk may be attributed to the tendency of larvae 10 mm standard length to approach the surface to ingest a bubble to fill the gas bladder (Hunter and Sanchez, 1977). The night to day ratio of catches is likely due to enhanced ability to react effectively to the slow approach (70 cm/sec) of the CalCOFI net in daytime.

Stage Duration

The duration of fixed arbitrary developmental stages of fish larvae controls the estimation of mortality. If all adjacent stages of fish larvae are of identical duration, a precise and accurate estimate of mortality rate is possible from relative estimates of abundance of the adjacent stages. For example, if one stage is twice as long as the following stage, the interstage mortality rate will be overestimated owing to the relative overestimate of the first stage. Of course, mortality "inversions" can occur when the second stage is so long as to appear more abundant than the first. Unbiased mortality rate estimates may be possible if stage duration is known.

1. Temperature

Temperature can influence mortality estimates over time or area by delaying larval development in colder time periods or areas leading to a longer duration at a stage and an overestimate of relative abundance. Temperature and natural variation may be the exclusive controls on development rate and stage duration in the embryonic period (before feeding) of the larvae. In anchovy the embryonic development period may be doubled by a change from 18°C to 13°C, leading to a twofold overestimate of abundance at that stage.

2. Food

Following total utilization of the yolk, the rate of feeding and energy expended searching for food may markedly influence the duration of predefined stages. No studies of the effect of feeding on duration of predefined stages have been completed. It may be assumed that variability by a factor of 2 in duration may occur in the early larval stages, and a factor of 7 seems possible for the later larvae. However, this high level of variability does not appear to be supported by the age distributions of larvae caught at sea (Methot and Kramer, 1979).

Statistical Tranformation

It seems possible to confuse the graphic (Bagenal, 1955; Aitchison and Brown, 1966) and analytical properties of the exponential decline in abundance with the statistical properties of log transformation. It is, of course, permissible as a first approximation to plot the logs of abundance versus time to obtain a linear form of the exponential mortality and to interpolate on this basis. A problem arises if, instead of plotting the log values of the stage sample means, one plots the means of the logs of the sample values. This is the geometric mean, and the use of adjacent values of the stage geometric means will lead to a bias in the estimate of mortality slope. This bias originates from either or both of two sources related to the dispersal or aggregation of the larvae—changing sample variance and changing sample coverage.

1. Sample variance

The geometric sample mean is a function of the arithmetic mean and the sample variance. Thus changes in the geometric mean have imbedded in them changes in both sample mean and variance. The general trend of mortality in larvae is also accompanied by dispersal of patches in the embryonic and early larval stages and the appearance of reaggregation in the later larval stages. The effect is that the geometric mean is a large underestimate of abundance in the more patchy embryonic stage and a smaller underestimate of abundance in the more dispersed early larval stage; a mortality rate calculated from geometric means will thus be an underestimate of the population mortality rate. Such a comparison of geometric means may even result in changing the sign of the mortality rate. Less serious perhaps in the late larvae would be the tendency for the bias of the geometric mean to be greater in a late stage, and this would mathematically induce an overestimate of mortality brought on by the reaggregation of the population into patches.

2. Log transformation

Two approaches to log transformation arise in the treatment of zero samples: (1) if one adds a constant to all sample values before transformation and (2) if we analyze positive samples only. When analyzing mortality of fish larvae, addition of a constant induces a gradual decrease in the slope owing to the larger proportionate contribution to the total of the constant. Secondly, the dispersal of the embryonic stages entails expanding coverage of the habitat, possibly reducing the number of "zero" samples for a time and changing the proportionate contribution of the added constant. Analysis of only positive samples under these same conditions results in an overestimate of the mortality rate. For different species of larvae, I consider it prudent to examine these effects before proceeding with analysis of mortality. Alternately, methods not employing logarithms could be used.

3. Weighted negative binomial

The weighted negative binomial model (Bissell, 1972; Zweifel and Smith, in press) can be used to obtain unbiased sample means and maximum likelihood estimates of the upper and lower confidence limits. The advantage of this model has no biological basis but is related to the explicit treatment of "zero observations," the use of the arithmetic mean as one parameter, and the ability to accommodate all scales and intensity of contagion from Poisson distribution to log-normal.

Sampling Strategy

Limited resources for collection of larvae at sea, sorting, identifying and measuring on land, and analysis of the data lead one to consider questions of sample strategy. From examination of CalCOFI data used for biomass assessment, one may gain some insight into sampling requirements for more specific hypotheses regarding larval mortality. Some preliminary considerations of the extent of sampling and the temporal and spatial intensity of sampling may be deduced from existing survey data. The CalCOFI surveys usually covered tens to hundreds of thousands of square nautical miles, with one station for each 800–1600 square nautical miles. Surveys were at monthly or quarterly intervals, and annual estimates of species abundance were formed from 1500–2000 samples. This data set has limitations at the smaller scale for determining sampling strategy, but the scale of patches is probably from 0.2 to 1 nautical square mile (the size and movement of a spawning school) and the period of vulnerability of larvae to a plankton net is of the order of three weeks. For this purpose we will consider six hypothetical larval mortality situations: larval transport, critical period, predation (including cannibalism), starvation, preschooling distribution, and spawning condition.

Larval Transport

The null hypothesis is "changes in geographic distribution of the larvae relative to the geographic distribution of spawning have no important influence on the numbers of fish which survive to become mature." To test this, one needs an estimate of the number of survivors from the cohort of interest and a set of larval samples. This set of samples must be spatially intensive to provide an estimate of mean position at several stages of larvae in the embryonic, early, and late larvae stages. The sample set for northern anchovy would also need to be temporally and spatially extensive because of the long duration and wide area of spawning from which the survivors eventually emerge. Space-time units for anchovy could be several hundred square miles at biweekly or monthly intervals from December to July. Within each space-time unit there would be sufficient precision for a useful mortality estimate from fewer than 100 samples.

Critical Period

The null hypothesis is "larval mortality is constant for all stages of embryonic larvae and early larvae, or there is a gradual improvement in survival as the larvae differentiate sensory and locomotor structure." The term "critical period" is an aquarist's phrase for the transition from rearing yolked larva stages to those requiring the provision of the proper kind and amount of food. It is reasonable to assume that first-feeding is also important in nature. The demonstration of this phenomenon at sea should probably begin with temporally intensive sampling over a small area near the maximum concentration of larvae. Because the embryonic stages and the early larval stages which ensue are still highly aggregated following the schooled spawning, adequate precision of estimates of the mean and standard error of the mean will require 500–1000 samples taken with sufficent precaution to eliminate escapement or extrusion through the meshes at the time of hatching. Mesh size should be 0.333 mm for northern anchovy, and the total volume filtered should be kept low to minimize variance.

Predation

The null hypothesis is "species 'A,' which coincides in space and time with the anchovy eggs or larvae, does not prey on the anchovy to such an extent that the anchovy egg or larva mortality rate is appreciably changed." In the test of this hypothesis, one requires spatially intensive samples which are adequate to sample both predator and prey. For example, in the special incidence of "cannibalism" it was found necessary to deploy plankton nets with 0.333 mm mesh and in the same area to deploy commercial-scale trawls to capture the adults. Other predators could require intermediate net sizes or could be obtained from the same samples as required to determine the larval mortality rate. To assemble a model of changes in larval mortality rate as a function of changes in the coincident populations of predators, the quantitative deployment of several scales of samples is required. It does not seem likely that population models for predators will be necessary on this time scale.

Starvation

The null hypothesis is "in nature the larval mortality rate is not affected by the amount, kind, spatial distribution, and production of food organisms." To gather evidence for this hypothesis, one would need the usual spatial and temporal intensity of sampling required to define larval mortality and the ability to sample with high spatial definition the food of the anchovy larvae. This would require the coupled deployment of sampling equipment with sufficient retention capacity to retain the food of the larval anchovy. The food samples would need only to cover the spectrum of sizes below the sampler used for the larval samples. The smallest size of interest is determined by the acuity of the larval eyes, and the largest size of interest is determined by the gape of the larval mouth. Since the larval mortality rate needs to be monitored for several months, one needs population models of the prey organisms to estimate food production. Another aid in resolving the horizontal and vertical dimensions of spatial intensity would be a series of models concerning the formation and destruction of food aggregations. Also, the changes in larval growth under various conditions of starvation will be required to adjust the size-specific mortality rate and the time-specific mortality rate estimates.

Preschooling Distribution

The null hypothesis is "in nature there are no important regional or temporal changes in dispersal rate which would materially influence the rate of formation of schools by juvenile anchovy." The tests of this hypothesis would require verification of the size and number of juvenile fish schools as a function of the distribution and number of fish larvae from which the schools were formed. Like the "predation" hypothesis, this would require a wide range of sampling apparatus. The deployment would be different in that the predation test requires simultaneous samples while the "preschooling distribution" hypothesis requires a sequential arrangement of samples of various sizes. For example, plankton nets or pumps would be deployed for the larval mortality rate, 60 days later micronekton net samples of juveniles would be needed, and later still, commercial size samples of prerecruits and adults would have to be taken. Sample repetition and the resultant sample variance would be used to evaluate the intensity of aggregations. Determining the scale of aggregation would require high spatial intensity and continuity for resolution.

Spawning Condition

The null hypothesis is "within the observed range of physiological condition of spawning adults, there will be no important changes in the subsequent survival rate of larvae." This test would require samples of the adult anchovy for six months prior to the spawning season and temporally intense samples of the egg production and larval survival.

Conclusions

While many plausible hypotheses exist to explain the variation in survival rate of larvae and the rate of addition of young fish to the commercial stock, there have been few tests. The scarcity of tests of hypotheses is caused by the lack of identification of the spatial and temporal intensity needed for samples required for the tests of single hypotheses. The evaluation and comparison of two or more mechanisms is far more difficult, and multiple tests are likely to be necessary. This may be stated as a null hypothesis, "the fundamental cause of variation in the survival of anchovy from spawning to recruitment is the same from year to year."

Larval Anchovy Patchiness

In the previous section I pointed out how larval anchovies have been used to assess biomass. Underlying this technique is the recognition that the larvae occur in patches and that a knowledge of the causes of patchiness is central to applying this technique. An investigation of larval survival must take into consideration patchy distribution of larvae as well. Anchovy larval patchiness has many origins, among them schooling of spawning adults (Smith, 1978b), diurnal periodicity in spawning behavior, local sites of high larval mortality, dynamic oceanic events like convergence zones, and larval aggregation behavior. Unfortunately, it has not been possible to study these contributing causes to patchiness in sufficient detail to detect the importance, scale, and consistency of the causes of patchiness (Fasham, 1978).

Schooling of Adults

The adult northern anchovy is found in schools, but it is not known whether schooling is a necessary condition for survival. Mais (1974) reported several years of surveys with a sonar using the "sonar mapping" technique (Smith, 1970), which yields an estimate of the number of schools per unit area and an estimate of the distribution of school sizes. Table 2 is a summary of measured targets from all seasons in the California Dept. of Fish and Game Surveys (Mais, 1974). From this table it is seen that about 94 percent of all fish schools are less than 80 meters in diameter, but if school tonnage is proportional to school cross-sectional area, the 6 percent of schools larger than 80 meters in diameter contain more than half the anchovy biomass.

Seasonal data from Mais (1974), summarized in Table 3, show that the number and size of anchovy schools increase rapidly in summer and fall. There is reason to believe that the additional schools may contain radically less biomass (⅓ to ½) per unit surface area (Hewitt et al., 1976, Fig. 4b; Vent et al., 1976, Figs. 7d and 7e). These may not be spawning schools. Instead, they may be the large schools of loosely compacted juveniles spawned in the preceding fall, winter, and spring.

Anchovy schools are probably more compact in the daytime (when we have measured the schools with sonar) than they are at night when they are spawning. For example, the average daytime compactness of 15,000 grams of anchovy per square meter of school horizontal area (Hewitt et al., 1976) could have 7500 grams of female anchovy of which one-sixth (1250) are spawning; 380 eggs per gram of female would yield 475,000 eggs per square meter per night (Hunter and Goldberg, 1980). Our largest samples of eggs are about one-twentieth of this value, or 23,750 eggs per square meter. This value will have been influenced not only by the spawning school becoming less compact at night, but also by gross motion of the school during several (6–8) hours of spawning and by turbulent dispersion of the eggs following spawning and fertilization.

Spawning and schooling behavior in the Pacific sardine is probably analogous to that of the northern anchovy. A localized analysis of 183 plankton samples (from Smith and Richardson, 1977, p. 84) is shown in Table 4. The major features of the development of larval patchiness following spawning are shown. One characteristic is that there are 85 percent positive samples of first-feeding larvae (5 mm SL) and only 66 percent positive samples of first-day eggs. Owing to dispersion, more area appears to be covered by larvae than by eggs. In about three weeks, there have been increases in unit sample areas covered by 2, 8, 32, 128, and 512 sardines per 10 m² and decreases in areas with 0, 8, 192, and 32,768 sardines per 10 m². By the time the larvae are 10 mm long, there are no sample counts of 128 and above, and only 20 percent of the unit sample areas contain larvae.

Last, it should be noted that a condition of random distribution where the variance equals the mean is not attained in the set of data in Table 4. The variance:mean ratio is 11,840 to 1 for first-day eggs and is still 15 to 1 for 10 mm larvae. Unfortunately, we have insufficient observations to determine how much of the patchiness persists from the nocturnal spawning behavior of the adults and, alternately, how much of the larval distribution is the result of pattern-forming activities such as localized areas of high mortality, aggregation behavior of the larvae, and dynamic ocean events like convergence.

Statistical Consequences of Larval Patchiness

The primary statistical consequence of larval patchiness is the requirement for large numbers of samples to allow an estimate of absolute abundance with useful levels of precision. The number of samples required for a constant precision of ±10% of the mean for the 3 days and sardine larvae to 10 mm length are shown at the bottom of Table 4. The range is from 6,759 samples of first-day eggs to 1,093 samples of 5 mm larvae. The rapid increase in samples with no larvae in the 8, 9, and 10 mm classes imposes additional sampling requirements.

Although the trends in sampling requirements by stage of development look reasonable, one should be cautious about the actual values, because the parameter estimates are sample estimates from only 183 samples. The actual number of samples required is a function of the population mean and the population variance, not the sample mean and variance. Current estimates of sample mean and variance are also likely to include sources of variance other than larval patchiness (English, 1964) such as temporal and spatial gradients

Table 2. Anchovy school diameter frequency distribution by school and biomass.

School diameter (m)	School biomass (metric tons)	Frequency	Sample proportions	Cumulative sample proportions	Class biomass (metric tons)	Biomass proportions	Cumulative biomass proportions
10	1.2	9,906	0.4338	0.4338	11,670	0.0274	0.0274
30	10.6	9,002	0.3942	0.8281	95,447	0.2245	0.2519
50	29.45	1,822	0.0798	0.9079	53,662	0.1262	0.3782
70	58	706	0.0309	0.9388	40,755	0.0959	0.4740
90	95	824	0.0361	0.9749	78,631	0.1849	0.6590
110	143	178	0.0078	0.9827	25,374	0.0597	0.7187
130	199	217	0.0095	0.9922	43,204	0.1016	0.8203
150	265	50	0.0022	0.9944	13,254	0.0312	0.8515
170	340	40	0.0018	0.9961	13,619	0.0320	0.8835
190	425	51	0.0022	0.9983	21,690	0.0510	0.9345
210	520	19	0.0008	0.9992	9,871	0.0232	0.9577
230	623	7	0.0003	0.9995	4,362	0.0103	0.9680
250	736	3	0.0001	0.9996	2,209	0.0052	0.9732
270	859	1	0.0000	0.9996	859	0.0020	0.9752
290	991	2	0.0001	0.9997	1,982	0.0047	0.9799
310	1,132	1	0.0000	0.9998	1,132	0.0027	0.9825
330	1,283	3	0.0001	0.9999	3,849	0.0091	0.9916
350	1,443	0	0.0000	0.9999	0	0.0000	0.9916
370	1,613	0	0.0000	0.9999	0	0.0000	0.9916
390	1,792	2	0.0001	1.0000	3,584	0.0084	1.0000

Table 3. Selected parameters of northern anchovy schools in California coastal waters (calculated from Mais, 1974).

Season	Anchovy schools (no/km²)	Anchovy school size (m²/school)	Coverage $\dfrac{\text{m}^2 \text{ of anchovy school}}{\text{m}^2 \text{ surveyed}}$
Winter	0.79	1151	0.0009
Spring	0.73	772	0.0006
Summer	1.22	1327	0.0016
Fall	1.98	1683	0.0033

(Colebrook, 1969) and regional and seasonal differences in abundance and survival. All data analyzed so far (Smith, 1972; Parker, 1980) indicate that the schooling pattern of the adults is the major source of variance.

Because schools are the major source of variance, any regional or seasonal correlative studies or analyses of variance must expend a high level of sampling effort to ascertain cause and effect of survival and environmental conditions. Log-transformation does not materially aid these comparisons. For example, in Table 4, the geometric mean provided by log-transformation increased from 23 stage "A" eggs to 40 5-mm larvae, while the arithmetic mean decreased from 673 stage "A" eggs to 161 5-mm larvae. It is mathematically possible to estimate the arithmetic mean from the mean and variance of log-transformed data, but there are insufficient studies to date to establish the efficacy of estimating two parameters, mean and variance of the log-transformed sample values, to further estimate another population parameter, the arithmetic mean. This statistical phenomenon should be explicitly solved by simulation before cause and effect studies are planned and conducted at sea.

It is apparent that the variance of numbers of eggs and larvae in samples is a result of the interaction of the size of the sample and the size of the patch. For example, patchiness on the scale of centimeters would not be measurable with a 1-meter net towed several meters. One obvious solution to sample variance would be to lengthen the tow until the proper proportion of larval patch to low-density areas between patches is obtained in a single sample. For this tactic to succeed there should be one scale of patch constant from place to place and from time to time.

It is not yet possible to test the consistency of patch scales; it is known that patchiness occurs on several broadly differing scales at sea. Smith (1970) reported a school group, believed to be northern anchovy, about 10 km in diameter. Fiedler (1978) reported the analysis of several school groups detected by California Dept. of Fish and Game Sea Surveys. The mode of school group radii detected was 8 miles (13 km) and the distribution ranged from 2 to 64 miles (3–100 km), with a log normal distribution with parameters $\overline{\ln x}$ = 2.319 and variance 0.676. Within school groups, the number of schools per

Table 4. Sample frequency distribution of Pacific sardine eggs and larvae and number of samples required to obtain a standard error of the mean of 10% (modified from Table 3.17, Smith and Richardson, 1977).

		EGGS (Days post-spawning)			LARVAE (Standard length, mm)						
ln(X+1)	X	A	B	C	3	5	6	7	8	9	10
0	0	65	44	76	29	27	38	57	91	124	146
1.1	2	7	14	5	13	5	12	23	21	32	23
2.2	8	14	14	16	36	20	32	51	52	19	12
3.5	32	20	27	31	50	46	68	45	18	8	2
4.9	128	36	33	17	29	49	30	7	1		
6.2	512	22	25	26	23	34	3				
7.6	2048	12	21	12	3	2					
9.0	8192	6	5								
10.4	32768	1									
$\bar{X}$		673	557	225	129	161	43	15	6	3	1
S_x		2,823	1,433	515	298	272	75	26	13	7	4
S^2_x		7,968,421	2,054,393	264,757	88,524	73,756	5,574	668	170	46	15
Required samples to obtain standard error of mean = $\frac{\bar{X}/1.96}{10}$		6,759	2,544	2,009	2,004	1,093	1,158	1,141	1,814	1,963	5,762
Percent positive		66	76	58	84	85	79	69	50	32	20

square mile exhibits a mode at 67 (20/km²) and the distribution ranges from 9 schools to 221 schools per square mile (3–64/km²). The log normal parameters are $\overline{\ln x}$ = 3.910 and variance 0.510. School sizes exhibit a mode at 10 meters and a range of distribution of from 0 to 400 meters (Mais, 1974, Table 1). Also, the compaction of fish within the schools (Hewitt et al., 1976) varies from 0.25 to 64 kg/m2, with a mode of 4 kg/m² and a log-normal distribution with parameters $\overline{\ln x}$ = 1.952 and variance 1.916. Graves (1977) photographed within fish schools at sea and detected a range of 50–366 fish per square cubic meter (Fig. 9). The underlying importance of the intensities and scales of contagion is that it is unlikely that a sample tow of any particular fixed length will diminish sample variance materially.

Biological Consequences of Larval Pattern

For fish schooled as adults, larval pattern may represent only a brief dispersed interlude in the life cycle. Some of the advantages of schooling as an adult could be conferred on the larval aggregations. Shaw (1978) lists the advantages of schooling as follows: conservation of energy while swimming through hydrodynamic interaction; enhanced reproductive opportunity; improved learning; greater tolerance of toxic substances; and protection from predators. Probably only improved learning and protection from predators would apply to the larval stage.

Protection from predators (Brock and Riffenburg, 1960; Hobson, 1978) through aggregation is implemented by decreased probability of contact and this is most advantageous when the size of the aggregation is adequate to satiate the predator. This latter consequence may operate at the larval stage or the maintenance of aggregations in the larval stage may only facilitate the formation of schools of "viable" size following metamorphosis into schooling juveniles.

Hewitt (1981) has considered the adaptiveness of larval pattern and described the life-cycle pattern through the larval stage for two fishes, the clupeiform anchovy (Engraulidae, *Engraulis mordax*), and the perciform jack mackerel (Carangidae, *Trachurus symmetricus*). He finds that the spawning pattern is less intense for the perciform. An index of patchiness indicates that the pattern becomes identical for anchovy and jack mackerel after two weeks of age.

Our interest in patchiness and particularly the changes in patchiness from one life stage to another stems from the conviction that since mean abundance of older larvae so far does not allow the distinction to be made between highly successful and moderately successful year classes, it may be that the intensity of pattern rather than mean abundance controls the success of survival in the later stages. With this rationale, the maintenance of patches in the larval state secures the advantages of schooling far sooner for the juveniles.

Lastly, patchiness may be a requirement for survival. Vlymen (1977)

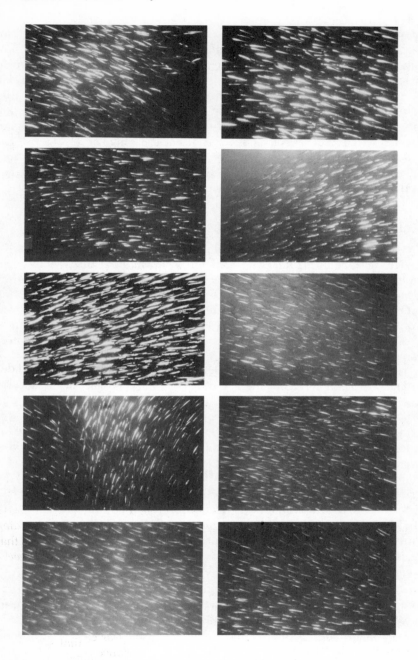

Figure 9. Portions of anchovy schools photographed at sea (Graves, 1977) with the Isaacs-Brown free vehicle drop camera. The mean of ten schools was estimated to be 115 fish per cubic meter (standard deviation 99, range 50–366, median 69).

demonstrated with a simulation model that larval growth requires patchiness in its food given the quantity of food in the sea. Thus a major oceanographic feature may be the stability to foster and maintain patches of food and permit the larvae to remain in favorable patches (Hunter, 1976; Lasker et al., 1970; Smith and Lasker, 1978; Lasker and Zweifel, 1978; Hewitt, 1981). Possibly one of the more enduring effects of the CalCOFI program has been the transition from regarding patchiness as a statistical nuisance to the appreciation of pattern as a necessity in the pelagic ecosystem.

References

Ahlstrom, E.H. 1954. Distribution and abundance of egg and larval populations of the Pacific sardine. U.S. Fish. Bull. 56:82-140.

———. 1959. Vertical distribution of pelagic fish eggs and larvae off California and Baja California. U.S. Fish. Bull. 60:106–146.

———. 1965. A review of the effects of the environment of the Pacific sardine. Interntl. Comm. for No. Atlantic Fish., Spec. Publ. No. 6, pp. 53–74.

Ahlstrom, E.H. and J. Radovich. 1970. Management of the Pacific sardine. In A Century of Fisheries in North America (ed. N.G. Benson), p. 183. Spec. Publ. No. 7, Amer. Fish. Soc., Washington, D.C.

Aitchison, J., and J.A.C. Brown. 1966. The Lognormal Distribution. Cambridge Univ. Press.

Bagenal, M. 1955. A note on the relations of certain parameters following a logarithmic transformation. J. Mar. Biol. Ass. U.K. 34:289–296.

Bakun, A., and C. Nelson. 1977. Climatology of upwelling related processes off Baja California. Calif. Coop. Oceanic Fish. Invest. Rep. 19:107–127.

Bissell, A.F. 1972. A negative binomial model with varying element sizes. Biometrika 59:435–441.

Brock, V.E., and R.H. Riffenburgh. 1960. Fish schooling: a possible factor in reducing predation. J. Cons. int. Explor. Mer 25:307–317.

Colebrook, J.M. 1969. Variability in the plankton. Progr. Oceanogr. 5:115–125.

English, T. Saunders. 1964. A theoretical model for estimating the abundance of planktonic fish eggs. Rapp. P.-v. Réun. Cons. int. Explor. Mer 155:174–182.

Fasham, M.J.R. 1978. The statistical and mathematical analysis of plankton patchiness. In Oceanography and Marine Biology—An Annual Review, Vol. 16. Aberdeen Univ. Press.

Fiedler, P.C. 1978. The precision of simulated transect surveys of northern anchovy, *Engraulis mordax*, school groups. U.S. Fish. Bull. 76:679–685.

Graves, J. 1977. Photographic method for measuring spacing and density within pelagic fish schools at sea. U.S. Fish. Bull. 75:230–234.

Hayashi, S. 1961. Fishery biology of the Japanese anchovy, *Engraulis japonica* (Houttuyn). Bull. Tokai Reg. Fish. Res. Lab., 31:145–268.

Hewitt, R.P. 1981. The value of pattern in the distribution of young fish. ICES Symp. on Early Life History of Fish, Woods Hole, Mass., April 1979. Rapp. P.-v. Réun. Cons. int. Explor. Mer 178:229–236.

Hewitt, R.P., P.E. Smith, and J. Brown. 1976. Development and use of sonar mapping for pelagic stock assessment in the California Current area. U.S. Fish. Bull. 74:281–300.

Hobson, E.S. 1978. Aggregating as a defense against predators in aquatic and terrestrial environments. *In* Contrasts in Behavior (ed. E.S. Reese and F.J. Ligher), Wiley & Sons, New York.

Hunter, J.R. 1976. Culture and growth of northern anchovy *Engraulis mordax* larvae. U.S. Fish. Bull. 74:81–88.

Hunter, J.R., and C.K. Sanchez. 1977. Diel changes in swimbladder inflation of the larvae of the northern anchovy *Engraulis mordax*. U.S. Fish. Bull. 74:847–855.

Hunter, J.R., and S. Goldberg. 1980. Incidence of spawning at sea and fecundity in the multiple spawning fish *Engraulis mordax*. U.S. Fish. Bull. 77:641–652.

Kramer, D., M. Kalin, E. Stevens, J. Thrailkill, and J. Zweifel. 1972. Collecting and processing data on fish eggs and larvae in the California Current region, NOAA Tech. Rep. NMFS CIRC-370.

Lasker, R., H.M. Feder, G.H. Theilacker, and R.C. May. 1970. Feeding, growth and survival of *Engraulis mordax* reared in the laboratory. Mar. Biol. 5:345–353.

Lasker, R., and J.R. Zweifel. 1978. Growth and survival of first-feeding northern anchovy larvae *(Engraulis mordax)* in patches containing different proportions of large and small prey. *In* Spatial Pattern in Plankton Communities (ed. J.H. Steele), pp. 329–353, Plenum, New York.

Lenarz, W.H. 1971. Modeling the resource base. *In* Symposium on the Development of the San Pedro Wetfish Fishery—a Systems Approach (ed. A.R. Longhurst). Calif. Coop. Oceanic Fish. Invest. Rep. 15:28–32.

————. 1972. Mesh retention of larvae of *Sardinops caerulea* and *Engraulis mordax* by plankton nets. U.S. Fish. Bull. 70:839–848.

Lloyd, M. 1967. Mean crowding. J. Anim. Ecol. 36:1–30. MacCall, A.D. 1974. The mortality rate of *Engraulis mordax* in southern California. Calif. Coop. Oceanic Fish. Invest. Rep. 17:131–135.

Mais, K.F. 1974. Pelagic fish surveys in the California Current. Calif. Dept. Fish and Game, Fish Bull. 162, 79 pp.

Methot, R.D. Jr., and D. Kramer. 1979. Growth of northern anchovy, *Engraulis mordax*, larvae in the sea. U.S. Fish. Bull. 77:413–423.

Murphy, G.I. 1966. Population biology of the Pacific sardine *(Sardinops caerulea)*. Proc. Calif. Acad. Sci. 4th Series, 34:1–84.

Murphy, G.I., and R.I. Clutter. 1972. Sampling anchovy larvae with a plankton purse seine. U.S. Fish. Bull. 70:789–798.

Parker, K. 1980. Direct estimation of spawning frequency and spawning biomass in a multi-spawning pelagic species. U.S. Fish. Bull. 78:541–544.

Shaw, E. 1978. Schooling fishes. Amer. Sci. 66:166–175.

Slobodkin, 1962. Growth and Regulation of Animal Population. Holt, Rinehart and Winston, pp. 168.

Smith, P.E. 1970. The horizontal dimensions and abundance of fish schools in the upper mixed layer as measured by sonar, p. 563. *In* Proc. of an Int. Symp. on Biol. Sound Scattering in the Ocean (ed. G.B. Farquahar). MC Rep. 805, Dept. of Navy.

————. 1972. The increase in spawning biomass of the northern anchovy, Engraulis mordax. U.S. Fish. Bull. 70:849–874.

————. 1973. The mortality and dispersal of sardine eggs and larvae. Rapp. P.-v. Réun. Cons. Perm. int. Explor. Mer 164:282–292.

————. 1978a. Biological effects of ocean variability: time and space scales of biological response. Rapp. P.-v. Réun. Cons. int. Explor. Mer 173:117–127.

————. 1978b. Precision of sonar mapping for pelagic fish assessment in the California Current. J. Cons. int. Explor. Mer 38:31–38.

Smith, P.E., and S.L. Richardson. 1977. Standard techniques for pelagic fish egg and larva surveys. FAO Fish. Tech. Paper No. 175, Rome.

Smith, P.E., and R. Lasker. 1978. Position of larval fish in an ecosystem. Rapp. P.-v. Réun. Cons. int. Explor. Mer 173:77–84.

Smith, P.E., L.E. Eber, and J.R. Zweifel. In press. Large-scale environment events associated with changes in the mortality rate of the larval northern anchovy. ICES Symp. on Early Life History of Fish, Woods Hole, Mass., April 1979. Rapp. P.-v. Réun. Cons. int. Explor. Mer 178.

Smith, P.E., and C.A. Haight. 1980. A time series of age composition and apparent abundance of the northern anchovy, *Engraulis mordax*, with inferences about the strength of recruitment. SWFC Admin. Rep. LJ-80-07.

Theilacker, G.H. 1980. Changes in body measurements of larval northern anchovy, *Engraulis mordax*, and other fishes due to handling and preservation. U.S. Fish. Bull. 78:685–692.

Vent, R.J., I.E. Davies, R.W. Townsen and J.C. Brown. 1976. Fish school target strength and doppler measurements. Naval Undersea Center, San Diego, Ca., NUC Tech. Paper No. 521, 32 pp.

Vlymen, W.J. 1977. A mathematical model of the relationships between larval anchovy *(Engraulis mordax)* growth, prey microdistribution, and larval behavior. Env. Biol. Fish. 2:211–233.

Zweifel, J.R., and P.E. Smith. In press. Estimates of abundance and mortality of larval anchovies (1951–1975): application of a new method. ICES Symp. on Early Life History of Fish, Woods Hole, Mass., April 1979. Rapp. P.-v. Réun. Cons. int. Explor. Mer 178.

Feeding Ecology and Predation of Marine Fish Larvae

John R. Hunter

The objective of my three lectures in this series is to describe some of the behavioral and physiological characteristics of marine fish larvae that affect their survival and growth. The two major sources of larval mortality are probably starvation and predation. The first two lectures deal with feeding ecology of marine fish larvae; I point out differences in life history strategy and how such differences affect the ability of larvae to avoid starvation. These two lectures came from a review I had written in 1977 (Hunter, 1980), and that review is reproduced here with only minor changes. In my last lecture I discuss the problem of predation on eggs and larvae and make some general conclusions. In all lectures, I depend on my research and that of colleagues at the Southwest Fisheries Center in La Jolla, California.

Feeding Ecology

Parental Effects

Egg Size, Yolk Quantity, and Starvation

The size of a larva at the time of first feeding and the amount of time available to find food before onset of irreversible starvation are largely determined by the maternal influence of egg size and by water temperature. Shirota (1970) found that the length in millimeters of 40 species of marine and freshwater larvae at onset of feeding was related to egg diameter in millimeters by the simple relationship L = 4D. Large size at onset of feeding is an advantage because larger larvae are able to swim faster and search a greater volume of water for food.

As shown in Table 1, larvae from large eggs generally have more time to find food before the onset of irreversible starvation, because yolk persists for a longer period after feeding begins and the larvae have greater reserves in their body which can be used in metabolism (Blaxter and Hempel, 1963). Larvae from small pelagic eggs are capable of existing for about 1–2 days after yolk absorption before onset of irreversible starvation, whereas larvae from large eggs such as herring and plaice are able to exist for 6 days after yolk absorption, and in grunion larvae starvation is still reversible after 16 days (May, 1971). The ability to withstand starvation increases steadily from this point. At the beginning of metamorphosis, herring can withstand 15 days, plaice 23 days (Blaxter and Ehrlich, 1974), anchovy 14 days, and Pacific mackerel larvae 5 days (Hunter, 1976b; Hunter and Kimbrell, 1980a). These differences reflect in part differences in activity; plaice are less active than herring at this time (Blaxter and Ehrlich, 1974) and anchovy less than mackerel. Differences between older fishes reared in the laboratory must be considered only in a relative sense because of the striking differences in condition between reared and wild animals (Blaxter, 1975).

The duration of egg incubation, although strongly affected by temperature, is also influenced by egg size. Ware (1975) found the relationship between the incubation time (I; days) at the water temperature for peak spawning and egg diameter (D; mm) for 14 species of Northwest Atlantic fishes was D = 0.101 I + 0.67. Similarly, the duration of the yolk sac stage is also affected by egg size (Blaxter and Hempel, 1963). Thus, larger eggs improve the survival capabilities of a larva at the onset of feeding, but at the

Table 1. Vulnerability to starvation of eight marine fish larvae at the time of first feeding.

Species	Temp. °C	Length mm	Dry weight μg	Yolk absorption Period days	Days to point of no return[a] relative to: Hatch	Days to point of no return[a] relative to: Yolk absorption	Days to point of no return[a] relative to: Onset of feeding
GRUNION[c]							
Leuresthes tenuis	20	9.0	362	4	12 + [b]	8 + [b]	12 + [b]
CLYDE HERRING[d]							
Clupea harengus	7–8	8.2	189	8	25	6	22
HADDOCK[e]							
Melanogrammus aeglefinus	7	3.5	—	6–7	6	0–1	—
PACIFIC MACKEREL[f]							
Scomber japonicus	19	3.1	40	3	4.0	1.0	1.6
NORTHERN ANCHOVY[g]							
Engraulis mordax	16.5	2.9	21	4	7.7	1.5	2.5
BAY ANCHOVY[h]							
Anchoa mitchilli	24	2.5	18	1.7	3.1	1.4	1.7
SEA BREAM[h]							
Archosargus rhomboidalis	22	2.3	28	2.2	3.4	1.2	1.7
LINED SOLE[h]							
Archirus lineatus	24	1.9	22	3.3	3.8	0.5	1.3

[a] Time of irreversible starvation (Blaxter & Hempel, 1963).
[b] 50% mortality from starvation, not a point of no return, because all survivors able to survive if fed.
[c] May (1971).
[d] Blaxter & Hempel (1963); Blaxter & Ehrlich (1974).
[e] Laurence (1974); Laurence & Rogers (1976).
[f] Hunter & Kimbrell (1980).
[g] Lasker et al. (1970); Hunter (unpubl. data).
[h] Houde (1974); Houde (1978).

cost of decreasing fecundity and increasing the duration of stages most vulnerable to predation.

The optimum egg size must strike a balance between numbers and the risks of starvation and predation. At lower temperatures, where incubation periods are longer, the advantage generally falls to larger eggs, whereas the reverse appears to be true at higher temperatures (Ware, 1975). Fine adjustments in these tactics appear to exist within a species to meet seasonal and regional differences in environment. Egg size varies significantly among spawning groups of herring (Blaxter and Hempel, 1963) and is known to vary seasonally in many species, with the largest eggs produced in the spring at the coolest temperatures and egg size declining as the season progresses (Bagenal, 1971; Ware, 1975).

The estimation of days to irreversible starvation has generally been made from the time of complete yolk absorption, but the time from onset of feeding provides more insight to survival strategy, as most larvae begin to feed before the yolk is completely exhausted. Herring larvae have a prolonged period in which they are capable of feeding but still have yolk (Table 1). The thermal optimum in efficiency of yolk utilization is another possible larval adaptation to specific environmental conditions. Sea bream larvae retain more yolk at the onset of feeding at 26°C than at other temperatures and thus have more yolk to sustain them if food is not present (Houde, 1974). Plaice larvae have a sharply defined thermal optimum in yolk utilization efficiency between 6.5°C and 8°C, which if realized could produce larvae 10 percent larger at the time of first feeding (Ryland and Nichols, 1967).

Spawning Tactics

Eggs of pelagic spawners are often distributed in extremely patchy patterns; 37% of Pacific sardine eggs taken in the years from 1951 to 1959 occurred in only 0.6% of the samples (Smith, 1973). Helfrich and Allen (1975) found the density of mullet eggs, *Crenimugil crenilabis*, to be 17 eggs/l at the surface after about one or two seconds of intensive spawning. A high density of northern anchovy eggs taken in a neuston net was 31 eggs/l, corresponding to a density of 46,000 eggs per 10 square meters of sea surface, which is in the upper 5% of all samples of anchovy eggs collected with nylon nets (unpublished data, NMFS, Southwest Fisheries Center, La Jolla). Other high egg densities include 31,000 eggs per 10 square meters for Pacific sardine (Smith, 1973) and 9,000 eggs per 10 square meters for Atlantic mackerel (Sette, 1943).

The eggs in such patches gradually disperse; dispersion is more rapid at the perimeter of the patch, resulting in a denser centrum surrounded by a less concentrated corona. The horizontal mean distance between neighboring eggs increases in a patch from one to two centimeters at spawning to 15–20 cm in most several-day-old sardine eggs (Smith, 1973). In northern anchovy, dispersion of larvae as measured by the negative binomial K (Lloyd, 1967) continues from hatching until the larvae attain a length of about 10 mm, at which time they reach their most dispersed stage and contagion increases thereafter (J. Zweifel, unpublished data, NMFS, Southwest Fisheries Center, La Jolla). This change from decreasing to increasing contagion coincides with the time anchovy begin nightly migrations to the sea surface to fill their swim bladders (Hunter and Sanchez, 1976) and is close to the onset of schooling, which begins at about 13 mm. Vertical migration may set the stage for schooling by concentrating larvae near the surface at night and thus increasing the frequency of social contacts.

Dispersion of larvae could progress to the point where it might influence onset of schooling or delay formation of schools of viable size. *Menidia* larvae reared in isolation took more time to form a school when brought together than socially reared larvae, and the length of the delay was proportional to the period of isolation (Shaw, 1961). Breder and Halpern (1946) showed that *Brachydanio rerio* larvae reared from the egg in isolation were quite hesitant to join a school. Thus, onset of schooling could be retarded if larvae are dispersed to the point where social contacts are infrequent.

Intraspecific competition and cannibalism also may be affected by initial spawn density and dispersion rates. Houde (1975) found that growth and survival of sea bream decreased rapidly when stocking density exceeded 8 eggs/l at food levels of 1500–3000 microcopepods/l. Food concentrations of 100 microcopepods/l did not sustain sea bream larvae except at stock densities of 2 eggs/l. Bay anchovy larvae *(Anchoa mitchilli)* seem to be much less affected by stock density (Houde, 1975, 1977). Sibling cannibalism is common in rearing larvae of large piscivorous fishes such as the scombroids (Mayo, 1973), but is unreported and presumably rare in clupeoid fishes. Thus, larger and more active larvae seem to be more cannibalistic and competitive for food and possibly better able to find schooling companions because of faster swimming speeds. Formation of dense patches of eggs and slow dispersion rates may favor clupeoid larvae, but lower egg densities may be more favorable to the more active larvae.

Swimming Behavior

Swimming during the yolk-sac stage consists of bouts of continuous, very energetic swimming followed by relatively long periods of rest. This behavior appears to be common in many small marine yolk-sac larvae but has been described in detail for only the northern anchovy (Hunter, 1972; Weihs, 1980). This mode of swimming in anchovy larvae is energetically advantageous for yolk-sac anchovy larvae because water viscosity is the dominant factor when larvae are in this stage (low Reynolds number). When larvae reach 5 mm, the Reynolds number is sufficiently high that beat and glide swimming becomes the more economical mode (Weihs, 1980).

After conclusion of the yolk-sac period, the cruising speed of larvae becomes of major importance in their feeding ecology, because it affects the frequency that larvae encounter prey and also accounts for the greatest metabolic expenditure. Swimming of larvae in this period may also differ somewhat from adults, due in part to the lack of mechanical support of the caudal fin and to the low Reynolds number (Weihs, 1980). Tail-beat amplitude and tail-beat frequency are continuously modulated in northern anchovy larvae (Hunter, 1972) and Pacific mackerel larvae (Hunter and Kimbrell, 1980a), whereas in adult fishes amplitude is modulated less frequently, except during accelerations (Hunter and Zweifel, 1971). Because tail-beat frequency is inversely proportional to length in fishes (Bainbridge, 1958; Hunter and Zweifel, 1971), the frequency in early larval stages can be quite high, reaching 50 beats per second in 4–5 mm anchovy and Pacific mackerel larvae. At their cruising speed, anchovy larvae use a beat and glide mode of swimming similar to that of adults. This mode of swimming is slow and thereby reduces the volume of water that can be searched, but it has a high metabolic efficiency—25% in a 14 mm larva (Vlymen, 1974).

Temperature can have a major effect on activity or cruising speed. Two effects of temperature on activity are illustrated in Figure 1 for northern anchovy reared to age 12 days at various temperatures on a diet of *Gymnodinium splendens*. Temperature affected the timing of the transition from the

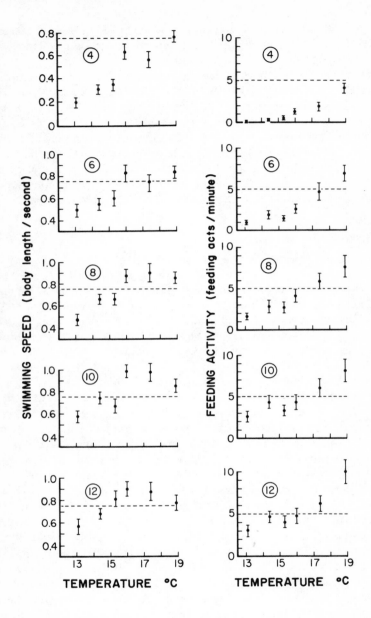

Figure 1. Effect of temperature on swimming speed and feeding rate of northern anchovy fed *Gymnodinium splendens* (mean density 400 cells/ml). Points are means, bars are 2 × standard error of mean, panel numbers are larval age in days, and dashed line is a visual reference. Data based on direct visual observation of larvae for 5 min. intervals. Each point average of value for 15 fish in two or more rearing groups.

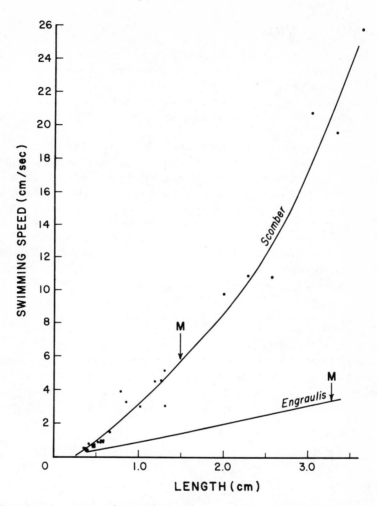

Figure 2. Swimming speed of Pacific mackerel, *Scomber japonicus*, larvae and juveniles at 19°C; points are means for five or more observations; curve fit by eye; and swimming speed of northern anchovy larvae, *Engraulis mordax*, at 17°C–18°C from Hunter (1972). Speeds are total distance covered including time spent in rest and feeding, and M indicates fish length at metamorphosis.

inactive yolk-sac stage to the active feeding stage as well as having a direct effect on activity of older larvae. At age 4 days, negligible feeding activity occurred in larvae at 15°C or lower, and the speed-temperature relation was a function of developmental rate. At ages 8–12 days, all larvae were past this transition. A direct effect of temperature on activity is evident in the figure.

Cruising speeds increase markedly over larval life more or less in proportion to length. Blaxter and Staines (1971) observed that the cruising speed of herring larvae increased from 20 cm/min at the end of yolk-sac stage to 80 cm/min 8 weeks later; in pilchard (*Sardina pilchardus*) speed increased from 10 to 30 cm/min in 3 weeks; in plaice from 10 to 60 cm/min over 7 weeks; and in sole (*Solea solea*) from 5 to 40 cm/min over 7 weeks. They also noted that cruising speeds of flatfish, sole, and plaice dropped by 90% at metamorphosis. Similarly, oxygen consumption of winter flounder, *Pseudopleuronectes americanus*, was shown by Laurence (1975) to decline sharply at metamorphosis.

Specific comparisons in activity or swimming speed from the literature are difficult to make because of differences in temperature, methodology, and lack of data on larval size. Data collected in my laboratory on anchovy and mackerel show that anchovy larvae swim more slowly than mackerel larvae at all stages of development (Fig. 2). Such a striking specific difference in cruising speed is diagnostic of major differences in life history tactics because it implies marked differences in searching abilities and metabolic requirements. For example, at 18°C, anchovy larvae consume 4.5 μl O_2/mg dry wt/hr, whereas mackerel consume 6.1 μl O_2/mg dry wt/hr (Hunter, 1972; Hunter and Kimbrell, 1980a). The actual difference in metabolic rate between these species is probably greater because the larvae were confined in small Warburg flasks which probably reduced the activity.

Blaxter (1969) concluded from his review that cruising speeds of larval fishes are on the order of 2–3 body lengths/sec and burst speeds (speeds that can be maintained for a few seconds) are on the order of 10 body lengths/sec. The cruising speed of anchovy is close to 1 body length/sec, and in mackerel it increases from 2 to 3 during the larval stage. Thus, these two speeds approach the upper and lower limits of the general range of cruising speeds.

Feeding Behavior

Prey Perception and Recognition

Marine fish larvae are visual feeders. All those studied so far—plaice, herring, and anchovy—lack rods and retinomotor pigment migration during the first weeks or months of life (Blaxter, 1968a, 1968b; O'Connell, 1981). That feeding is confined to daylight hours is also indicated by stomach content analysis in other species (Arthur, 1976).

To be perceived, a prey must be relatively near; first-feeding herring larvae react to prey at 0.7–1.0 body length L (Rosenthal and Hempel, 1970) or 0.4L (Blaxter and Staines, 1971), plaice at 0.5L, and pilchard at 0.2L (Blaxter and Staines, 1971). Ninety-five percent of the prey reacted to by northern anchovy were within 0.4L of the axis of progression (Hunter, 1972).

It would be unreasonable to attach much importance to differences between species among these values. The factors controlling perceptive ranges in larval fishes have not been studied, and size of prey was not isolated as a variable. In adult planktivorous fishes, perceptive distances appear to be a linear function of prey size (Confer and Blades, 1975). If perceptive distances increase with prey size in larvae, this would certainly increase the effective searching volume of larvae specializing in such prey. In all these studies, the authors point out that perceptive ranges increase as larvae grow. Rosenthal and Hempel (1970) concluded that perceptive ranges in herring larvae also change with activity level, being greater during slow meandering swimming and shorter during faster swimming. They also state that herring larvae do not perceive prey which are beneath the plane of the horizontal axis of the body, but this does not appear to be the case for nothern anchovy larvae (Hunter, 1972).

The stimuli eliciting prey capture have not been studied in larval fishes, but in adult fishes prey size is usually the strongest factor, with movement seeming to direct attention of the fish toward the prey (Kislalioglu and Gibson, 1976a). Almost all predators which are believed to depend upon prey movement are able to detect prey even when it is motionless (Curio, 1976). The frequent occurrence of copepod eggs and other nonmotile foods in the stomachs of field-caught larvae and *Artemia* eggs and other nonmotile foods in laboratory-reared larvae (May, 1970) clearly shows that movement is not essential in many species. Prey size selection so dominates selection patterns in larval fish that it is difficult to evaluate the role of other prey characteristics such as spines and other protective structures, color, or avoidance behavior. Bowers and Williamson (1951) concluded that some copepods with spiny appendages, such as *Acartia*, occur in the stomachs of herring larvae less frequently than would be expected from their abundance in the plankton, and Arthur (1976) suggested that jack mackerel may select the more brightly colored copepods such as *Microsetella*, which occur in their stomachs in greater abundance than seen in the plankton. It would be of considerable interest to study such characteristics under controlled laboratory conditions from the standpoint of both larval feeding ecology and copepod evolution.

Motor Patterns

Upon sighting a prey, a clupeoid larva forms a sinuous posture and advances toward the prey by sculling the pectoral fins and undulating the finfold while maintaining the body in the S-posture. When the prey is a short distance from the snout, the larva opens its mouth, straightens its body to drive forward, and engulfs the prey (Breder and Krumholz, 1943; Rosenthal and Hempel, 1970; Hunter, 1972). Larvae of plaice, *Pleuronectes platessa* (Riley, 1966), and northern sennet, *Sphyraena borealis* (Houde, 1972), and other fishes are also reported to form a sinuous feeding posture, but the behavior has been studied in detail only for clupeoids and for the freshwater coregonid larvae, *Coregonus wartmanni* (Braum, 1967), and quite possibly differences exist among species.

Mackerel larvae, *Scomber japonicus*, feed in a manner more typical of the attack of many adult fishes. Upon sighting a prey, the larva advances toward the prey, stops, draws back the tail, and holds it in a slightly recurved high amplitude position (the C-start position of Webb, 1978). The rest of the body is straight; feeding is accomplished by opening the mouth and driving the tail posteriorly. Presumably many other larvae of similar robust body form feed in this way.

Anchovy larvae often form and reform the S-posture while maintaining their orientation to a moving prey; but my observations indicate that, once the strike is made, anchovy larvae rarely strike again at the same prey. Mackerel larvae, on the other hand, frequently strike two or more times at the same prey if the preceding strike was unsuccessful. Mackerel larvae often reposition for the second strike by moving backward; anchovy and other clupeoid fishes do not appear to have this maneuverability (Blaxter and Staines, 1971). Large prey are more difficult to capture and are less abundant in the sea; consequently, persistence in a feeding attack as exhibited by mackerel may be an essential characteristic of a species whose strategy depends on larger prey.

Webb (Paul Webb, University of Michigan, Ann Arbor, unpublished data) described in detail the starting postures of feeding pike and largemouth bass. He concluded that pike, which use an S-start as do anchovy larvae, are less persistent in the attack and strike at higher speeds and at shorter range than do bass, which use a C-start. The parallels between his observations and ours on mackerel and anchovy larvae seem obvious.

The time spent poised in a striking posture in anchovy larvae is much longer at the time of first feeding than in later larval life, and gradually the strike becomes integrated with swimming movements; the duration of complete feeding acts declines from 1.5–2.0 seconds to about 0.6 seconds when larvae reach 17 mm, and relative speed of the strike also declines (Hunter, 1972). The poised stereotyped striking posture (C- or S-starting position) seems to be a common tendency in young larvae and becomes integrated into swimming movements as the larva grows, and suggests that it may be an adaptation to feeding on relatively large and fast prey. As will be shown subsequently, young anchovy larvae feed on much larger prey relative to their size than do older larvae.

Handling times are negligible when copepods and other small zooplankton are prey because the prey are engulfed by the mouth instantaneously. Piscivorous fish larvae manipulate their prey, and consequently handling times increase with prey size as is the case for adult fishes (Kislalioglu and Gibson, 1976b). The appearance of piscivorous habits requires development of a new set of motor patterns associated with grasping prey and presence of a sufficient number of teeth to accomplish this end. Larvae of the northern sennet, *Sphyraena borealis*, usually seize other larvae crosswise and, by a successive series of head shakes, move the grasp to either the head or the tail. Then without losing grip, the prey is swallowed head or tail first (Houde, 1972). Houde observed that newly hatched fish larvae were eaten by sennets at age 10 days and were the preferred food of sennets 9 mm and longer. I observed the same behavior in the Pacific barracuda, *Sphyraena argentea*, feeding on siblings in a rearing tank. In this case, piscivorous feeding began at age 5 days when larvae were only 4.4 mm. Pacific mackerel larvae become piscivorous when they reach 10 mm. They also seize other larvae from the side, carry them crosswise in the mouth, periodically release the prey, and grasp it again until it dies. Then they release it and ingest it, usually head first.

Feeding Success

Feeding success of fish larvae is often low at the onset of feeding. Estimates for herring are 6% (Rosenthal and Hempel, 1970) and 2%–6% (Blaxter and Staines, 1971), for coregonid larvae 3%–5% (Braum, 1967), and for northern anchovy 10% (Hunter, 1972). Feeding success gradually increases, reaching 90% in about 3 weeks in anchovy (Hunter, 1972) and in about 7 weeks in herring (Blaxter and Staines, 1971). In contrast to these species, plaice larvae capture 32%–62% of prey attacked at the onset of feeding (Blaxter and Staines, 1971), and the relatively large larvae of *Belone belone* (12 mm) capture 60%–100%, depending on prey type (Rosenthal and Fonds, 1973).

Blaxter and Staines (1971) suggest that the initially high success of plaice larvae may be due to increased maneuverability of plaice relative to herring and to their ability to swim backwards. Feeding success of anchovy larvae dropped from 80% to 40% at age 17 days when the prey was changed from *Brachionus* to *Artemia* nauplii, but in 2 days their success increased to the former level (Hunter, 1972). Changes in mouth size or other developmental changes could not occur so rapidly, thus the difference appears to be attributable to experience.

Searching Behavior

Food density requirements have been estimated from behavioral search models of the basic form outlined by Ivlev (1960). These models in their simplest form require an estimate of ration, swimming speed, perceptive field, and feeding success, with many other parameters added as complexity increases. These models range in complexity from the simple models of Rosenthal and Hempel (1970), Blaxter and Staines (1971), and Hunter (1972), where only basic parameters are considered, to the increasingly complex models of Jones and Hall (1974) and—the most complex to date—Vlymen (1977). Vlymen's model is the only one that does not assume a random search pattern and that addresses the problem of a contagious food distribution. In his model the larvae have no effect on food density, and the model does not use a prey-size-dependent modulation of perceptive field and feeding success. All such models are extremely sensitive to assumptions regarding the perceptive field and swimming speed and to the accuracy of these measurements. For example, Blaxter and Staines (1971) estimated that the searching abilities of herring larvae increase from 0.1 to 2.4 l/hr over 8 weeks, whereas Rosenthal and Hempel (1970) estimated they increase from 1.5 l to about 10 l/hr in 10 weeks. The major difference in these results is in the differences in perceptive distances and rates of swimming (Blaxter and Staines, 1971). It would seem to be of value to use such models to set up hypotheses that could be tested in the laboratory or at sea.

Owing to these problems and to effects of temperature, specific comparisons are difficult, but these estimates do suggest that the volume searched by young larvae is often quite small: pilchard (5–7 mm) search 0.1–0.2 l/hr, plaice (6–10 mm) search 0.1–1.8 l/hr (Blaxter and Staines, 1971), and anchovy (6–10 mm) search 0.1–1.0 l/hr (Hunter, 1972). All studies show that searching abilities increase markedly with growth, since speed, capture success rates, and perceptive distances are functions of length or age.

In the two cases studied, search patterns in larval fishes were nonrandom. Larval anchovy decrease their speed and change their turning probabilities when they enter a dense patch of food. The probability of making a complete reversal in direction increased from 0.04–0.05 at low food densities to 0.23 in dense patches of *Gymnodinium* and to 0.07 in patches of *Brachionus* (Hunter and Thomas, 1974). Wyatt (1972) showed that the time plaice spent swimming increases with a decrease in food density. Similar nonrandom search patterns have been described for adult fishes (Kleerekoper et al., 1970; Beukema, 1968).

Prey

Prey Type

Naupliar through adult stages of copepods are the typical food of most marine fish larvae studied to date. Some notable exceptions to this rule exist: in the North Sea in normal years, the food of plaice larvae consists mostly of the appendicularian *Oikopleura dioica* (Shelbourne, 1962), and larval fishes may be a common item in the diet of the more piscivorous larvae. Larvae are commonly eaten by larval Pacific barracuda (Ahlstrom, personal communication, NMFS, Southwest Fisheries Center, La Jolla) and blue marlin, *Makaira nigricans* (Gorbunova and Lipskaya, 1975); and judging by high incidences of cannibalism under rearing conditions, they may be frequently eaten by many scombroid larvae (Mayo, 1973). Blue marlin larvae begin feeding on fish larvae at 6 mm, and they become the principal food by 12 mm (Gorbunova and Lipskaya, 1975). Under rearing conditions, the scombroid fishes, *Euthynnus alletteratus, Scomberomorus cavalla, Scomberomorus regalis*, and *Auxis* become cannibalistic at about 5 mm (Mayo, 1973), *Scomber japonicus* at 10 mm, and *Sphyraena argentea* at 4.4 mm (Hunter, unpublished data). Under aquarium conditions, sibling cannibalism appears to end as scombroid fishes become juveniles and begin schooling (Mayo, 1973; Clemens, 1956; Hunter and Kimbrell, 1980a).

Larvae tend to be more euryphagous during the earliest stages and often eat such organisms as tintinnids, phytoplankton, mollusk larvae, and ciliates as well as copepods (Arthur, 1976; Bowers and Williamson, 1951; Lebour, 1921; and Rojas de Mendiola, 1974). Phytoplankton, often identified as green remains, is relatively common in the stomachs of clupeoid larvae at about the time of first feeding but is uncommon soon after. In general, the use of phytoplankton in laboratory rearing studies as a sole source of food for first-feeding larvae has been unsuccessful (May, 1970). Northern anchovy, on the other hand, are able to subsist on a diet of the dinoflagellate *Gymnodinium splendens* for up to 20 days, but at a greatly depressed growth rate (Lasker et al., 1970; Theilacker and McMaster, 1971). Anchovy will feed on a variety of dinoflagellates, *Gymnodinium, Gonyaulax, Prorocentrum,* and *Peridinium,* but not small flagellates, *Chlamydomonas, Dunaliella,* nor diatoms, *Ditylum, Chaetoceros, Thalassiosira,* and *Leptocylindrus* (Scura and Jerde, 1977). That larvae fed *Gonyaulax* (40 μm diameter) did not survive, whereas those fed *Gymnodinium* (50 μm diameter) did, led Scura and Jerde to conclude that it is the small size of *Gonyaulax* which makes it an inadequate food. Using the same line of reasoning, it seems doubtful that any of the other dinoflagellates they studied would support growth because they are even smaller in diameter.

The tendency for larvae to feed upon a greater variety of organisms in early larval life and subsequent specialization in stages of copepods may simply be due to the existence in the sea of a greater variety of small organisms of the proper size. The ability to subsist on the relatively small organisms such as dinoflagellates may be restricted to larvae of relatively modest energy demand, such as the northern anchovy, i.e., a larva of relatively low initial weight, low activity, existent in cool water.

Prey Size

Size dominates prey selection patterns of larval fishes and is one of the best diagnostic characteristics for evaluating specific ecological roles. The critical dimension for ingestion of copepods and other oblong prey is the maximum width including appendages (Blaxter, 1965; Arthur, 1976). Evidence for this is based on the fact that copepods frequently found in the stomachs of larval fishes are too large to be ingested if length were the critical factor (Blaxter, 1965; Hunter, 1977). Copepods are usually found in the stomachs of clupeoid larvae with antennae folded back along the body (Blaxter, 1965). Blaxter goes on to say that copepods with antennae folded in such a way are probably the only ones that are captured successfully. Inclusion of the appendages increases the maximum width of adult and copepodite stages by about 49% in *Pareuchaeta,* and 25% in *Calanus, Pseudocalanus, Acartia, Microcalanus,* and *Metridia,* but has a negligible effect in *Temora, Oithona, Oncaea,* and *Microsetella* (Wiborg, 1948a).

The increase in size of prey selected by marine fish larvae as they grow is well documented in the literature and occurs in every species studied. Often, prey length or life stage was used as a measure of size rather than the more informative measurement of maximum prey width. A striking feature of

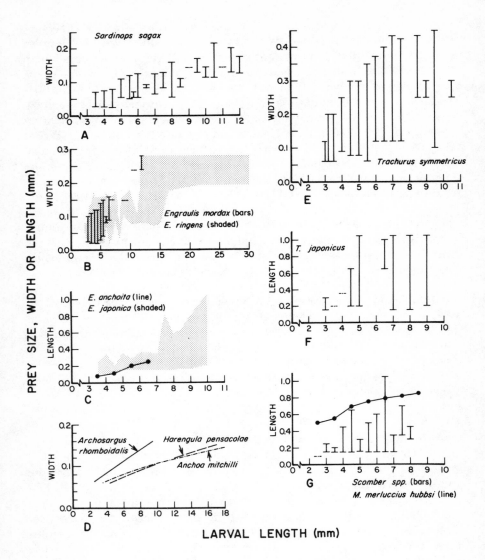

Figure 3. Relation between prey size and larval length for 12 species of marine fishes; label on ordinate indicates whether prey width or prey length were measured; vertical bars and shaded areas represent range of prey sizes; and straight lines connecting dots indicate average prey sizes. Plots were redrawn from Arthur (1976) for *Sardinops sagax*, *Engraulis mordax*, and *Trachurus symmetricus*; from Rojas de Mendiola (1974) for *Engraulis ringens*; from Detwyler and Houde (1970) for *Harengula pensacolae* and *Anchoa mitchilli*; from Stepien (1976) for *Archosargus rhomboidalis*; from Ciechomski and Weiss (1974) for *Engraulis anchoita* and *Merluccius merluccius*; and from Yokota et al. (1961) for *Engraulis japonica*, *Trachurus japonicus*, and *Scomber* spp. Data were for sea-caught larvae except panel D, which were laboratory reared.

these data is the consistency of trends among related species and groups (Fig. 3). The small clupeoid larvae, *Sardinops*, *Engraulis*, *Harengula*, consistently feed on small prey of the order of 50–200 μm width; both species of *Trachurus* show a tendency for a marked increase in the range of food sizes eaten with length, and *Scomber* show a somewhat similar trend. In the three engraulid species, there appears to be a consistent tendency for a marked increase in the range of prey eaten between 8 and 12 mm. Hake larvae, *Merluccius*, begin feeding on much larger foods than the rest, with only a slow increase in average prey size. Ciechomski and Weiss (1974) point out that hake begin feeding on advanced copepodite and adult stages of copepods.

The consistency of these trends from different localities and species strongly suggests that these patterns are the result of positive size selection inherent in species or specific ecological groups of larvae. Stepien (1976) demonstrated that sea bream larvae select foods by size, with a slight positive electivity for prey of 100–200 μm width in larvae 4–5 mm and a stronger positive electivity for prey 200–300 μm in larvae 7–9 mm. The difference between sea bream and the two clupeoid larvae in the figure may be more marked under natural conditions, because the food size preference of sea bream increases faster than the increase in size of the food in the rearing tanks.

Except for hake, specific differences are less marked at the onset of feeding, with all larvae feeding on prey of 50–100 μm width, although jack mackerel take much larger foods as well. Houde (1973) remarks that organisms 50–100 μm are eaten by a great variety of larvae at this time, including those with relatively large mouths such as the tunas and flatfishes. Arthur (1977) estimated the naupliar biomass in the California Current system and expressed it in terms of naupliar width. The naupliar biomass was at a maximum between 50 and 80 μm of naupliar width and declined sharply on either side even though there were many more nauplii of smaller sizes. He points out that the food size ranges of first-feeding Pacific sardine, northern anchovy, and jack mackerel all overlap the naupliar biomass maximum, and it appears that the feeding range of many other larvae do so as well.

Larvae in the above comparisons are relatively the same size at onset of feeding and hatch from relatively small eggs. Larvae from large eggs, for example exocetid larvae and saury (*Cololabis saira*), are 6–7 mm at first feeding and feed on a range of prey equivalent to that of older jack mackerel or *Scomber* of about the same size (Yokota et al., 1961). None of the species in Figure 3, other than hake, could eat newly hatched *Artemia* nauplii at the onset of feeding, but rearing studies reviewed by May (1970) indicate that plaice larvae, two species of *Fundulus*, a species of *Sebastes*, two cottid species, four species of atherinids, *Aulorhynchus flavidus*, and *Fugu pardalis* feed successfully on *Artemia* nauplii at the onset of feeding. Many of these species have large eggs, again emphasizing the importance of the maternal contribution in the feeding tactics of some larvae.

An additional feature of importance in these records is the slow increase

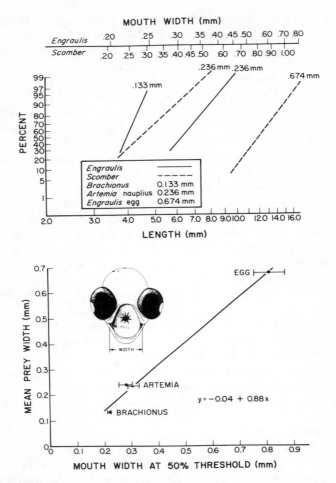

Figure 4. Relation between width of mouth and ability of *Scomber japonicus* and *Engraulis mordax* to capture prey of various widths. Upper panel, percent of larvae that captured one or more prey, shown as a function of mouth width (upper scales) and larval length (lower scale); lines are for the regression of probit on log larval length. Lower panel, average width of prey, shown as a function of the mouth width at which 50% of the larvae ingested one or more prey; estimates taken from probit lines given in upper panel; and bars are the 95% confidence intervals for the estimate. Density of prey in the experiments were: *Brachionus* 9/ml; *Artemia* 10/ml; and *Engraulis* eggs 10/l.

in the minimum size of prey eaten in all species. The effect of this is to greatly expand the prey range in larvae that select larger prey, and this has important energetic consequences. In summary, marine larvae select foods of increasingly larger size as they grow, but the average and range of sizes selected differ greatly among species and may be diagnostic of specific ecological roles.

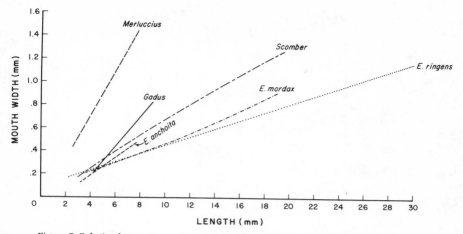

Figure 5. Relation between mouth width and larval length of hake, *Merluccius merluccius*, from Ciechomski and Weiss (1974); cod, *Gadus morhua*, from Wiborg (1948b); Pacific mackerel (*Scomber japonicus*) from Hunter and Kimbrell (1980a) and three species of anchovy, *Engraulis anchoita* from Ciechomski and Weiss (1974), *Engraulis mordax* from Hunter (1977) and *Engraulis ringens* from Rojas de Mendiola (1974).

Effect of Mouth Size

The size of the mouth and the rate it changes with length must be partially responsible for specific differences in food size selection. Shirota (1970) measured the gape of the mouth of 33 species of marine and freshwater larval fishes and correlated them with the size of natural foods and growth rates, and concluded that larvae with smaller mouths grow more slowly than those with larger ones. Blaxter (1965) showed that differences in gape of the mouth exist between different races of herring and concluded that these differences could be of great significance in early survival.

Mouth size would be expected to set the upper size limit for prey. To define this relationship, Hunter (1977) and Hunter and Kimbrell (1980a) determined for anchovy and Pacific mackerel the mouth size threshold for various prey. In these experiments, larvae were exposed to high densities of a single prey—*Brachionus*, *Artemia* nauplii, or anchovy eggs—for 2–4 hours, and the proportion of larvae that captured one or more prey was tabulated by mouth size classes. None of the larvae tested had any previous experience with the particular prey. The width of the mouth was closely correlated with the ability to capture these prey (Fig. 4). The first incidence of feeding occurred when the ratio of prey width to mouth width was close to unity with *Artemia* or anchovy eggs as the prey. In the case of *Brachionus*, it was lower (0.63), which may have been caused by the fact that first-feeding anchovy larvae were used in this experiment to avoid the effect of rapid improvement of success that occurs over the first few days.

These experiments indicated that, on the average, 50% of larval anchovy or mackerel were capable of feeding on these prey when the prey width to mouth width ratio was 0.76. The width of the mouth provided a good indica-

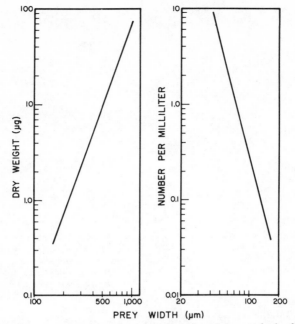

Figure 6. Left panel, relation between copepod width and dry weight (excluding nau-pliar stages) calculated from data given by Gruzov and Alekseyeva (1970). Right pa-nel, relation between number of prey per ml in the sea and prey width, recalculated from Vlymen (1977).

tion of the size of prey a larva is capable of ingesting. Mouth gape was also measured, but width was preferred because it can be measured with greater accuracy. A different relation could be expected for piscivorous feeding or when ingestion involved manipulation of the prey because larvae are capable of greatly expanding their mouths under these circumstances. The gape of the mouth would be expected to be related to handling time in this case (Kis-lalioglu and Gibson, 1976b).

These thresholds are of interest because they indicate how feeding success is affected by prey size. They also show that prey are eaten "end first" because at the lowest success levels the prey can be ingested in no other way. Many of the trends in size selection of prey discussed in the previous section are also suggested by the relationship between mouth width and length. The mouth sizes of the three engraulid species are similar to each other and differ markedly from those of the other species (Fig. 5). The mouth widths of all species but hake are somewhat similar in the beginning, but differences increase greatly with growth. Hake stands out as being distinctly different from the rest from the onset of feeding.

The sharp increase in food size that occurs in the engraulids between 8 and 12 mm occurs at a time anchovy become highly proficient in capturing *Artemia* nauplii, and the increase in prey size is to one of that diameter. No

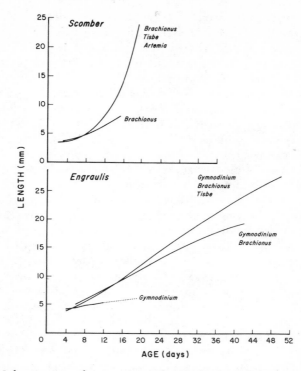

Figure 7. Laboratory growth rates using various foods of *Scomber japonicus* at 22°C from Hunter and Kimbrell (1980a), and of *Engraulis mordax* at 16°C from Hunter (1977). Caloric values of prey were: *Gymnodinium* 0.00005 cal; *Brachionus* 0.008 cal; and Artemia 0.0096 cal.

evidence exists from mouth size information to explain the leveling of food size that occurs thereafter despite the fact that the mouth continues to grow. It seems reasonable to assume larger prey would be eaten if the opportunity existed. Thus, other limits must be imposed; one such limit may be the slow swimming speed of engraulid larvae.

Nutritive Value of Prey of Different Sizes

The nutritive value of larger prey can be illustrated by considering the relation between width of copepods and their weight. Gruzov and Alekseyeva (1970) give a wet weight to length conversion for a group of copepods including species in Calanidae, Paracalanidae, Pseudocalanidae, and other families having a cephalothorax length-to-width ratio ranging from 2.0 to 2.8. I transformed their data to show dry weight as a function of cephalothorax width by using the midpoint of their width ratio (2.4) and assuming a water content of 87% (Lovegrove, 1966). This calculation indicated that an increase of 2.5 in copepod width produces an order of magnitude increase in dry weight. Thus, a larva feeding on copepodites 200 μm wide would have to capture ten times the number of prey to obtain the same ration as one feeding on cope-pods 500 μm wide (Fig. 6). The effect of a slight increase in width of prey eaten is more marked if the change from feeding on nauplii to copepodites is considered. The change in body width of *Calanus* from nauplius VI to cope-podite I is slight even when appendages are included in the measurement (Wiborg, 1948a), but the dry weight doubles. In *Calanus helgolandicus*, the dry weight of N.VI is 2.0 μg and that of C.I is 4.3 μg (Paffenhöfer, 1971). The well-known seasonal and regional variation in copepod weight (Marshall and Orr, 1955; Gruzov and Alekseyeva, 1970) should be considered in any study of food size relations in larval fishes.

The necessity for increasing prey size with growth is illustrated by com-paring growth rates of larval anchovy (Hunter, 1977) and Pacific mackerel fed different foods (Fig. 7). When anchovy are fed *Gymnodinium* alone, growth becomes asymptotic at about 6 mm, whereas when *Gymnodinium* and the rotifer *Brachionus plicatilis* are used, growth becomes asymptotic at about 20 mm and few larvae survive (survival drops from 46% at age 26 to 6% at age 42 days). Similarly, Pacific mackerel growth slows on a diet of only *Brachionus*, and few survive beyond 8 mm at age 15 days. Howell (1973) was able to grow plaice larvae through metamorphosis on *Brachionus* alone, but at a much slower growth rate than when *Artemia* was used, indicating that some species are able to grow through metamorphosis on rather small prey, but at a depressed growth rate.

Vlymen (unpublished data, NMFS, Southwest Fisheries Center, La Jolla) estimated for larval anchovy the minimum caloric value of prey required to meet energetic needs for parameters in his 1977 paper. The model uses a 12-hour feeding day, a temperature of 17°C, and the maximum feeding rate ob-served in the laboratory (about 10 attacks per minute). Gut capacity was not included, and consequently the limit was set by the maximum feeding rate. To calculate the minimum caloric value of prey necessary to meet energy needs, Vlymen used the model

$$E_1 + E_2 + E_3 + E_4 = 0.48R$$

where:

$E_1 = (5.10 \times 10^{-2}) L^{3.3237}$ (the basic metabolic rate in calories, where L = length in cm);

$E_2 = 0.19 L^{4.48}$ (the total energy cost of swimming);

$E_3 = 0.05 L^{4.48}$ (the total energy cost of feeding attacks at maximum rate during a 12-hour day);

$E_4 = 0.29R$ (the energy cost of mechanically processing food, intestinal propulsion, etc.); and

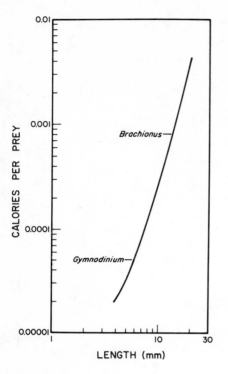

Figure 8. Relation between minimum caloric value of prey required to meet energy needs of larval northern anchovy at 17°C and larval length. From model developed by Vlymen (1977) and Vlymen (unpublished). The caloric value of *Gymnodinium* and *Brachionus* are indicated.

0.48R = the proportion of the ration R available for energetic needs.

The ration at the maximum attack rate was

$$R = (7.12 \times 10^3) \, C \times S$$

where 7.12×10^3 is the total number of attacks at the maximum rate in a day of feeding, C is calories per prey, and S is success of capture. By substitution he obtained

$$(3.78 \times 10^{-5}) \, L^{3.3237} + (1.77 \times 10^{-4}) \, L^{4.48} = C \times S.$$

The success of capture (S) is a function of age, not length, and is described by the function $S = 93.2 \log_{10} T - 33.3$, where T is larval age in days. To obtain the minimum caloric value of prey for larvae of various lengths, ages at specific lengths were obtained from laboratory growth rates (Hunter, 1976). The origin of the data and the derivation of the parameters used in this model are described by Vlymen (1977).

His results are reasonably close to those described above from rearing work. The model predicts no growth beyond a length of 6 mm on prey having a caloric value of *Gymnodinium* and none beyond 14 mm for *Brachionus*

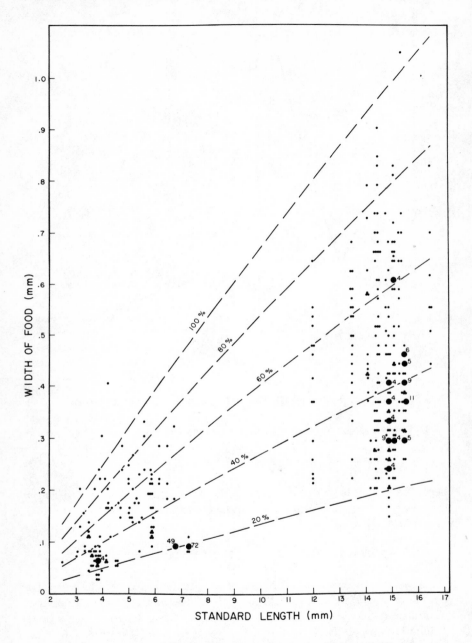

Figure 9. Width of foods eaten in the sea by Pacific mackerel larvae of various standard lengths. Each small point is the width of a single prey; larger points represent multiple points for prey of the same size and number observations. Dashed lines indicate the prey width equal to 20%–80% of the mouth width, or equal to the mouth width (100%), for mackerel larvae of 3–16 mm.

Table 2. Average[a] densities of microcopepods in the sea.

	Average density of microcopepods (number per liter)			
	nauplii	copepodites	total	Location
OPEN	13	2	15	Southeast Coast of Kyushu[b]
SEA	22	36	58[c]	California Current[c]
	40	5	45[c]	Southern California near shore[e]
	27	7	34[f]	Eastern Tropical Pacific[g]
	36	1	37	California Current[h]
PARTLY	76	19	95	Azov Sea[i]
ENCLOSED	—	—	223[j]	Gulf of Taganrog[k]

[a] Mean for all stations and years given in publication listed in table.
[b] Yokota et al. (1961)
[c] Includes all copepods passing 202 μm mesh net.
[d] Beers & Stewart (1967)
[e] Beers & Stewart (1970)
[f] Includes all copepods passing 202 μm mesh net and caught on 35 μm mesh.
[g] Beers & Stewart (1971)
[h] Arthur (1977)
[i] Duka (1969)
[j] Defined as food of *Clupeonella delicatula*; microcopepods account for over 90% of items eaten (Mikhman, 1969).
[k] Mikhman (1969)

(Fig. 8). Thus the lower size limit of prey, at least over the first few weeks of feeding, appears to be set by metabolic relations, whereas the upper limit is controlled by mouth size.

In the sea, many more small prey are eaten than large ones, even in large prey specialists such as Pacific mackerel larvae. Stomach contents of Pacific mackerel from the sea illustrate this point. The mean diameter of prey eaten by these larvae was about 40% of their mouth width (solid line, Fig. 9), although they were able occasionally to eat prey as wide as their mouth (Hunter and Kimbrell, 1980a). If one assumes the prey in Figure 9 to be spherical, which underestimates the size of the larger prey, the small prey that contributed 50% by number contributed only 10%–15% of the total volume of prey eaten. Thus the relatively large and rare prey probably make the major contribution to growth despite the fact that many more small prey are eaten.

Prey Abundance and Density Requirements

The density of particles in the sea declines rapidly with increasing size or diameter of the particle (Sheldon et al., 1972; Sheldon and Parsons, 1967). Such a relationship was presented by Vlymen (1977) for particle size distribution from Niskin casts measured with a Coulter Counter by Richard Eppley

Table 3. Food density thresholds for six species of marine fish larvae.

Species and common name	Container volume (liters)	Duration (days)	Food type	Stock density (No./L)	Survival at various food densities	
					Density (No./L)	Percent survival
PLAICE[a]						
Pleuronectes platessa	5	14	*Artemia* nauplii	50 (larvae)	1,000	72[b]
					500	72
					200	54
					100	32
NORTHERN ANCHOVY[c]						
Engraulis mordax	10.8	12	Wild zoo-plankton (nauplii)	10 (eggs)	4,000	51
					900	12
					90	0.5
					9	0
BAY ANCHOVY[d]						
Anchoa mitichilli	76	16	Wild zoo-plankton (nauplii-copepodites)[f]	0.5-2 (eggs)	4,700[e]	65
					1,800	50
					110	10
					60	5
					30	1
SEA BREAM						
Archosargus rhomboidalis	76			0.5-2 (eggs)	2,600[e]	75
					890	50
					130	10
					90	5
					50	1
LINED SOLE						
Achirus lineatus	38			0.5-2 (eggs)	610[e]	75
					220	50
					30	10
					20	5
					9	1
HADDOCK[g]						
Melanogrammus aeglefinus	37.8	42	Wild zoo-plankton (nauplii)	9[h] (larvae)	3,000	39
					1,000	22
					500	3
					100	0
					10	0

[a] Wyatt (1972).
[b] Survival was 100% at 50/L for first 7 days without a decrement in length; see also Riley (1966).
[c] O'Connell and Raymond (1970).
[d] Houde (1978).
[e] Estimated food density for indicated survival levels.
[f] Plankton blooms of *Chlorella* sp. and *Anacystis* sp. maintained in rearing tanks.
[g] Laurence (1974).
[h] Estimated by adjusting for hatching success.

(Scripps Institution of Oceanography, University of California San Diego, La Jolla) (Fig. 6). Sheldon et al. (1972) pointed out that roughly similar amounts of organic material exist in logarithmically equal size intervals in any water mass; hence, in any sample, many more small particles exist than large ones. This implies that to feed on larger prey, a larva must search a much greater volume of water, and it also may explain why the minimum and average prey sizes change slowly in larvae that select larger prey.

The density of particles in the size range relevant to larval marine fishes has been studied by a number of workers. Their results have been reviewed by Blaxter (1965), May (1974), and Arthur (1977) and are presented here in Table 2. These studies indicate that average density in the open sea is 13–40 nauplii/l and typically 1–7 copepodites/l. On the other hand, in enclosed areas such as lagoons, bays, and estuaries, much higher densities are found. Average densities in these areas of naupliar and postnaupliar stages combined can exceed 200/l.

Larval fishes have been maintained in the laboratory at various food densities to determine the density of prey required for survival. Some of these density experiments are summarized in Table 3. Most indicate that a prey density of 1,000–4,000 microcopepods/l is required for high survival rates in the laboratory. These results agree in general with what has become standard rearing practice in recent years; in such techniques, the highest densities are used initially and are subsequently reduced to about 1,000/l (Houde, 1973). Much higher densities are required for very small prey such as phytoplankton. Lasker (1975) found that anchovy larvae required 5,000–20,000 *Gymnodinium splendens* cells/l at 19°C and 20,000 or more at 14°C for significant feeding to occur. Standard rearing practice for northern anchovy requires 100,000 or more *Gymnodinium* cells/l (Hunter, 1976b), whereas 1,000 microcopepods/l appear to be adequate (O'Connell and Raymond, 1970).

Density thresholds determined by Houde (1975, 1977, 1978) are markedly lower than those of the others listed in the table and are substantially below those used for routine rearing of larval fishes. Houde attributes his lower thresholds to use of lower stocking densities, general improvement in culture techniques, and frequent daily monitoring and adjustment of food density. He also maintains a dense phytoplankton bloom in his containers, which may also contribute in some way to higher survival. Of particular interest is the very low threshold determined for sea bream, emphasizing the importance of specific feeding tactics. This species selects larger prey (Stepien, 1976) than the other species studied by Houde and, judging by the density threshold, is much more efficient in finding and catching prey.

In general the density thresholds determined for larvae in the laboratory are much higher than average microcopepod densities in the open sea, described in the preceding section. On the other hand, the high microcopepod densities in enclosed areas are within the range that Houde (1975, 1977) found to support survival and growth. Thus food may not be as critical for species such as those he studied, which exist in enclosed areas. Many problems exist in interpreting laboratory findings and extending them to field conditions. The interactions of stock density, food density, and mortality are problems which may be overcome to some extent by use of low stocking densities and frequent monitoring of food density. Changes in ration with development and prey size distributions in the tank are also critical. The few larvae that survive at very low prey densities may be those that captured, either by good fortune or because of a larger mouth, the few larger prey in the container. Selection of the appropriate criteria also poses problems. Growth as well as survival declines with food availability; this is evident in all the food density studies cited but perhaps best illustrated by Riley (1966), Wyatt (1972), and Houde (1975, 1977). Reduction of growth may be nearly as lethal as starvation because of the increased exposure to predation.

Patchiness

The disparity between most estimates of food densities required by larvae and average densities in the open sea has led to the hypothesis that larvae may be dependent on small-scale patchiness of food. In the sea, large-scale sampling will always tend toward the mean concentration between such patches. Data collected by Yokota et al. (1961) on naupliar abundance provide one of the better examples of patchiness of larval forage because the samples were taken on a scale relevant to larval searching behavior. They counted all the nauplii occurring in one-liter samples taken at the surface from an area off the southeast coast of Kyushu over two years. The average naupliar density for their 4,730 samples was 13/l. The greatest number in a single sample was 524, and only 2% of the samples accounted for over 20% of the nauplii.

Laboratory experiments on searching behavior discussed previously indicate that larva have the ability to remain in patches of food if they find them. The search model of Vlymen (1977) indicated that the average anchovy larva could not exist in the sea if food were distributed randomly. He concluded that first-feeding anchovy larvae require a food contagion of K = 0.17, where K is the negative binomial, just to meet minimum energy requirements. To meet minimum requirements, therefore, prey would have to be 1.3 times as "crowded" as they are on the average, if the population had a random distribution (Lloyd, 1967).

Lasker (1975) tested the patchiness hypothesis by exposing anchovy larvae to samples of water taken from the surface and from the chlorophyll maximum layers usually 15–30 m below the surface. Feeding by larvae was minimal in samples taken from the surface, but extensive feeding occurred in water from the chlorophyll maximum layer when these samples contained prey of about 40 μm at densities of 20,000–400,000 prey/l. The prey were primarily the phytoplankter *Gymnodinium splendens;* microcopepods were never at high enough densities to be eaten by the larvae. Houde and Schekter (1978) exposed sea bream to simulated patch conditions in the laboratory by increasing the concentration of microcopepods to 500/l for periods of 2–13 hours per day from a background density of 25–50/l. They found that survival at 10 days after hatching of larvae exposed to only three hours of food at 500/l was similar to that of larvae fed at a constant 500/l. Thus, even very short-term patchiness could enhance survival in this species. Lasker (1975) has considered a much broader time scale; the bloom of *Gymnodinium* had persisted for at least 18 days until a storm obliterated the chlorophyll maximum layer. His measurements after the storm indicated that the density of food was insufficient for feeding.

If patchiness of food is a key to larval survival in the open sea, one could expect survival and growth of larvae to show considerable small-scale patchiness within the species spawning region. Present evidence for northern anchovy larvae supports this view. O'Connell (1981) measured the incidence of starvation of larval anchovy in the sea using histological techniques that had been calibrated by starving larvae in the laboratory (O'Connell, 1976). He found that 8% of larval anchovy in the Los Angeles Bight in March were in poor histological condition, indicating that death from starvation was imminent. For larvae of the size he studied (about 8 mm SL) this could represent about 40% of the daily rate of mortality. Of great importance to this discussion is the high variability that existed in the condition of larvae occurring in different tows. In some tows, 60% of the larvae were starving, yet all larvae in tows taken a few nautical miles away were in excellent condition. Thus as much variability in starvation existed within a few nautical miles as existed over the entire Los Angeles Bight. Similarly, Methot and Kramer (1979) found as great a difference in growth of anchovy larvae (estimated from daily increments of otoliths) in samples taken a few nautical miles apart as among all samples taken in the Bight area. Thus larval foods, larval growth, and starvation all appear to exhibit small-scale patchiness. It may be the summation of such small-scale events over time and space that ultimately determines the success of a year class.

Predation

Little literature exists that is concerned specifically with predation on pelagic egg and larval stages of marine fishes. Many species within the major groups of pelagic invertebrates, including Medusae, Siphomedusae, Ctenophora, Chaetognatha, Cephalapoda, hyperiid amphipods, euphausiids, and carnivorous calanoid copepods, as well as pelagic fishes, have been reported to feed on the eggs and larvae of marine fishes. That predation exists is amply documented by food habit studies of organisms in these groups as well as by some aquarium observations, but most studies give no indication that the predation by a species is a significant part of natural larval mortality. The records of egg and larval predation are drawn primarily from general descriptions of food habits of the predators, and incidence of predation is often summarized without regard to the seasonal changes in larval and egg abundance. On the other hand, these studies indicate that larval fishes and eggs typically constitute a small and highly variable proportion of the foods usually eaten.

Estimates of mortality of egg and yolk-sac stages indicate that predation must be very high. Starvation can be eliminated as a source of mortality in these stages because larvae subsist on their yolk. Losses range from 10% to 95% per day and typically are 30%–40% (Jones and Hall, 1974; Vladimirov, 1975; Riley, 1974). Although predation is possibly the largest source of mortality in larval fishes, it remains at present largely undocumented.

In this lecture I will first discuss characteristics of the behavior of the parents and the larvae that affect vulnerability to predation and then consider the evidence for effects of specific marine predators. I restrict my presentation to predation in the pelagic realm, recognizing that predation on demersal eggs of marine fishes is often a major source of mortality. The larvae of many demersal spawners are pelagic, however, and may encounter the same groups of predators as those of pelagic spawners.

Factors Affecting Vulnerability

Parental Behavior

The spawning behavior of the parents affects the vulnerability of pelagic eggs and larvae to predation. These influences include the time and location of spawning and the density of eggs. Nocturnal spawning occurs in many clupeoids (Blaxter, 1970); in the northern anchovy, for example, spawning begins at sunset, reaches a maximum about midnight, and declines thereafter (Hunter and Goldberg, 1980; Hunter and Macewicz, 1980). Johannes (1978) concludes that the majority of tropical marine fishes with pelagic eggs spawn at twilight or night and suggests that this may reduce the intense predation by diurnal planktivores in tropical reef communities, because eggs are transported by currents into the open sea away from inshore planktivores. Hobsen and Chess (1978) reported that pelagic fish eggs are an important component of the diet of diurnal planktivores at Enewetak but were insignificant in diets of nocturnal planktivores. In the open sea, nocturnal spawning may also reduce vulnerability to predation because it permits some dispersion of egg patches before they become vulnerable to diurnal planktivores. The dense egg patches produced by clupeoid fishes may increase vulnerability because predators could converge on such patches and feed selectively on eggs and larvae.

Vulnerability to predators may also be reduced by the location of spawning. Johannes (1978) points out that many tropical reef fishes spawn in localities (on the outer reef slope, near channel mouths, in open water, and at other sites) where eggs are transported by currents away from the intense predation of the reef. Northern anchovy may spawn in areas in the open sea that have fewer large planktonic predators (Alvariño, 1980), a topic discussed in greater detail further on.

Starvation

It is generally believed that a prudent predator would select prey that are about to die anyway, that is, the youngest ones and those weakened by starvation or other causes. No information exists on the effect of starvation on vulnerability to predation of marine fish larvae, but one might expect it to vary with effect of starvation on sustained high-speed swimming. Laurence (1972) observed that the maximum speed that starved largemouth bass larvae, *Micropterus salmoides*, could sustain for 30 minutes declined with starvation, from about 3 to less than 2 body lengths per second, whereas the sustained speed of fed larvae was about 4–5 lengths per second. Ivlev (1961) in his classic work on the feeding ecology of fishes provides an example for freshwater juveniles and fry. Ivlev found that the effect of starvation on the vulnerability of roach fry to pike was strongly size dependent. Starvation of 10 cm roach fry had little effect on the vulnerability to predation by 12–15 cm pike, whereas predation doubled when 29 cm roach fry were starved. Ivlev goes on to say that the relation between starvation and vulnerability was similar in form to the swimming fatigue curve for roach fry (flow rate fish could sustain for 5 minutes), implying that a decrement of swimming ability caused by starvation was equivalent to a decrement in avoidance. An important conclusion that can be drawn from Ivlev's work is that the decrement in avoidance behavior caused by starvation is probably important only when the difference in size between predator and prey is not great.

Larval Size and Time of Day

Catch data from plankton nets illustrate that avoidance capabilities appear to increase exponentially with larval length. Murphy and Clutter (1972) compared the daytime catch of tropical anchovy, *Stolephorus*, taken in one-meter plankton nets with that taken at about the same time in a plankton purse seine. The ratio, purse seine catch to one-meter net catch, increased markedly with larval length after anchovy attained a length of about 5 mm (Fig. 10). The ratio of night catches in plankton nets to day catches follows a similar exponential trend with length in several other clupeoid fishes. That Murphy and Clutter's data for daytime avoidance are about the same as the day/night ratios for plankton net catches of clupeoids indicates that the apparent exponential form of the relation is not entirely the result of improvement in nocturnal vision. Recent work by Paul Webb (unpublished data, University of Michigan, Ann Arbor, Michigan) indicates that maximum speed of burst-swimming in anchovy larvae increases at a rate proportional to larval length times 20 and the duration of such bursts by length times 4. An explanation for the exponential increase in avoidance capabilities with length in clupeoid larvae is that avoidance is a function of both absolute speed and the duration that larvae are able to sustain that speed, as both factors increase with length; when combined they might yield an exponential relation.

In the more robust, fast-swimming larvae, such as jack mackerel and Pacific mackerel, day/night differences in catch are barely detectable. These larvae are able to escape almost as well by night as by day. The rapid decline of the catch curve of jack mackerel larval length in comparison with clupeoid larvae suggests that these more robust and fast-swimming larvae have a much greater avoidance ability (Lenarz, 1973). Few jack mackerel or Pacific mackerel larger than 7–8 mm are taken in routine oblique plankton tows (P. Smith, unpublished data, NMFS, Southwest Fisheries Center, La Jolla, Ca.).

Clupeoid larvae, as well as other species, do not develop a functional scotopic visual system until late in larval life (Blaxter, 1968a, 1968b; O'Connell, 1981); hence they would be more vulnerable to predators at night than in the day, as the day/night ratio of catch indicates. Murphy and Clutter (1972) also show that anchovy larvae avoid nets at night; however, detection of the net and perhaps predators at night, may be dependent on lateral line sense, because the lateral line is functional at hatching in anchovy (O'Connell, 1981). Vulnerability at night may also increase if larvae enter a less responsive state. Adult fishes have been shown to be less responsive to olfactory alarm stimuli at night than in the day (Thines and Vandenbussche, 1966). Anchovy fill their swimbladder at the water surface at night and remain relatively inactive, supported by the distended swimbladder until dawn (Hunter and Sanchez, 1976). Larval *Blennius pholis* survival was lower when maintained under continuous light than when given a daily light cycle (Qasim, 1959). These studies indicate existence of a diel rhythm in activity, and thus larvae might be less reactive to stimuli at night because of a different reactive state, but definitive evidence does not exist.

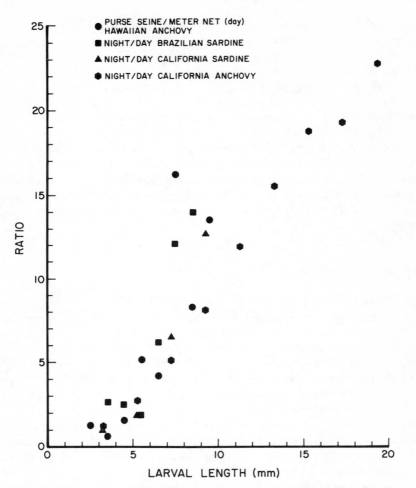

Figure 10. Change in avoidance ability of four species of clupeoid larvae with length. Avoidance ability indicated by the ratio of purse seine to 1-m net catches of the Hawaiian anchovy, *Stolephorus purpureus* (Murphy and Clutter, 1972); and by the ratio of night to day plankton net catches of the Brazilian sardine, *Sardinella brasiliensis* (Matsuura, 1977), California sardine, *Sardinops sagax;* and California anchovy, *Engraulis mordax* (Paul Smith, unpublished data, NMFS, Southwest Fisheries Center, La Jolla.)

State of Maturity

Maturation of sensory and locomotor systems must affect the ability of larvae to avoid predation. Although maturation continues throughout the larval phase, the greatest changes occur during the yolk-sac period. In northern anchovy larvae at hatching, innervation of the Mauthner cells is incomplete, the eye is nonfunctional (O'Connell, 1981), and activity consists of relatively long periods of rest, interrupted by brief periods of vigorous swimming (Hunter, 1972). By the end of the yolk-sac stage, innervation of the

Mauthner cells is complete, and the larva becomes capable of the rapid star-tle response of most teleosts (Eaton et al., 1977); the eye becomes functional for daytime vision, and the larva is almost continually active in the day. One would expect vulnerability to predators to decrease as these developmental events occur; this seems to be supported by laboratory evidence. The ability of copepods (Lillelund and Lasker, 1971) and euphausiid shrimp (Theilacker and Lasker, 1974) to capture yolk-sac larvae in the dark declined markedly over the yolk-sac period. For example, the feeding success of *Euphausia pacifica* declined from 60% for 1–2-day-old yolk-sac larvae to 17% for 3-day-old larvae and 11% for 4-day-old larvae. Theilacker and Lasker (1974) suggest that this decline is related to the increase in larval activity, because small predators such as copepods and euphausiids may be unable to capture moving prey and it is the long periods of rest that make larvae vulnerable to these predators.

Types of Predators

Planktonic Invertebrates

Consumption of marine fish larvae by marine copepods, euphausiid shrimps, hyperiid amphipods, and chaetognaths has been studied in small containers in the laboratory. Lillelund and Lasker (1971) showed that 11 species of calanoid copepods were capable of capturing or fatally injuring yolk-sac anchovy larvae. The number of yolk-sac anchovy killed by a *Labidocera jollae* female declined with larval age from 16 newly hatched larvae per day to about 7 for 168-hour-old larvae, and from about 5 larvae to 1 for *L. trispinosa* females. The median number of yolk-sac anchovy larvae eaten by the euphausiid shrimp, *Euphausia pacifica*, was 2 per day when the density of larvae exceeded 1 per 3,500 ml (Theilacker and Lasker, 1974); and at a density of 50 yolk-sac herring larvae/50 ml, the hyperiid amphipod, *Hyperoche medusarum*, attacked larvae at a rate of 0.45/hour (Westernhagen and Rosenthal, 1976). Two species of chaetognaths, *Sagitta elegans* and *S. setosa*, consumed on the average 1.5 fish larvae after a 48-hour starvation period, but larvae were not taken in significant numbers if the chaetognaths were not starved at least 24 hours (Kuhlman, 1977).

In *Sagitta* (Kuhlman, 1977) and *Labidocera* (Lillelund and Lasker, 1971), the number of larvae eaten or attacked was found to be independent of larval density as long as the density exceeded a certain minimum; on the other hand, in *Hyperoche* (Westernhagen and Rosenthal, 1976) and *Euphausia* (Theilacker and Lasker, 1974), the number of larvae attacked increased initially with larval density, then became asymptotic with density, the type two predator response of Holling (1966).

Probably only yolk-sac larvae are vulnerable to attacks of *Labidocera*, *Euphausia*, and *Hyperoche*, because older larvae easily avoided attack even in the small containers used in these studies. The two species of *Sagitta* are restricted to an even smaller size range because yolk-sac larvae were not attractive, presumably because of their lack of movement (Feigenbaum and Reeve, 1977), and larvae older than 4 days easily escaped. These small predacious invertebrates feed, of course, on foods other than fish larvae; the number of anchovy eaten by *Labidocera* declined in proportion to the density of the alternate food (*Artemia* nauplii), and *Sagitta* showed a strong preference for copepods when both copepods and larvae were offered (Kuhlman, 1977). *Hyperoche*, however, showed a strong preference for herring yolk-sac larvae over flatfish larvae.

It seems unlikely that *Sagitta setosa* and *S. elegans* have a significant impact on larval fish populations. In addition, Cushing and Harris (1973) conclude that chaetognaths are present in sufficient numbers to account for a larval mortality of only 1% per day. On the other hand, hyperiid amphipods, *Labidocera*, and *Euphausia* may be significant predators on yolk-sac stages of fish larvae. The first of the year populations of *Hyperoche* co-occur for 40 days with yolk-sac herring larvae, and fish larvae remains are the most abundant item in their gut (Westernhagen, 1976). In addition, Sheader and Evans (1975) report that fish larvae, especially *Clupea* and *Ammodytes*, make up 23.4% of the food of the hyperiid amphipod, *Parathemisto gaudichaudi*, during April and June. Both *Euphausia* and *Labidocera* co-occur with anchovy larvae along the California coast, but no food habit studies exist. Theilacker and Lasker (1974) estimated from the abundance of *Euphausia* and their median feeding rate in the laboratory that *Euphausia* could consume 2,800 anchovy larvae per day per square meter of sea surface, which is more than 40 times the average number of yolk-sac anchovy existent per square meter.

Certainly the potential predation by these small planktonic predators could have a significant effect on survival of early yolk-sac stages, but larger and more agile predators are required for older larval stages. Larger planktonic predators could include some of the larger Chaetognatha, Siphonophorae, Chrondrophorae, Medusae, and Ctenophora. No detailed studies on the impact of these larger invertebrate predators exist, although incidental observations of feeding behavior and food habit studies are available (Lebour, 1922, 1923, 1925; Frazer, 1969; and others).

Alvariño (1980) tabulated the abundance and co-occurrence with northern anchovy larvae of five major groups of large invertebrate predators— Chaetognatha (22 species), Siphnophora (48 species), Medusae (20 species), Ctenophora (4 species), and Chondrophorae (1 species)—taken in over 2,000 routine ichthyoplankton tows off the California coast in 1954, 1956, and 1958. In general, the abundance of all species combined showed an inverse relation to the abundance of anchovy larvae; that is, these potential predators were the most abundant in tows when anchovy larvae were not taken or were less abundant than average. To pursue this analysis further, she selected among the species those she felt to have the highest potential as larval predators because of their size, abundance, and feeding habits. These planktonic

Table 4. Most abundant large planktonic invertebrate predators taken in standard oblique plankton hauls along the California coast in 1954, 1956, and 1958 and their occurrence with larval anchovy (from Alvariño, 1980).

Abundance of anchovy larvae:	1954				1956				1958			
	High[a]		Zero		High[a]		Zero		High[a]		Zero	
Species abundance:	Frequency (%)[b]	Mean number[c]	Frequency (%)[b]	Mean number[c]	Frequency (%)[b]	Mean number[c]	Frequency (%)[b]	Mean number[c]	Frequency (%)[b]	Mean number[c]	Frequency (%)[b]	Mean number[c]
Chaetognatha												
Sagitta enflata	56	491.3	73	1093.7	43	191.8	47	121.6	74	271.6	82	308.4
S. hexaptera	22	5.5	55	16.1	27	1.8	53	62.0	26	15.5	52	42.2
S. scrippsae	33	48.1	52	19.2	20	3.2	33	17.4	16	6.5	27	9.9
Siphonophorae												
Stephanomia bijuga	7	0.2	27	0.8	13	1.2	22	2.0	11	0.2	27	1.8
Chelophyes appendiculata	33	10.0	76	89.3	17	5.0	47	7.6	32	2.6	67	46.2
Diphyes dispar	22	14.7	48	44.1	0	0	0	0	0	0	3	0.4
Medusae												
Liriope tetraphylla	22	20.9	64	253.6	37	96.5	42	41.8	21	6.8	58	89.4
Rhopalonema velatum	7	0.6	46	30.3	7	0.3	28	4.1	5	0.3	33	18.2
Aglaura hemistoma	0	0	12	40.2	0	0	3	1.1	5	0.2	18	51.7

[a] Greater than the average number of anchovy per positive haul (241 anchovy larvae per 10 square meters of sea surface).
[b] Percent of stations in which species occurred.
[c] Average number of individuals taken in positive stations.

predators occurred much less frequently and at lower abundances where anchovy were abundant and usually occurred most commonly where no anchovy larvae were taken (Table 4). The dominant constituents in collections where anchovy were abundant were copepods and euphausiids, whereas collections without anchovy were dominated by jelly-like plankters, salps, doliolids, and pyrosomes. Thus, anchovy spawn most intensely in areas where large planktonic predators capable of feeding on post yolk-sac larvae were rare and where foods for the adults and larvae were abundant (copepods and euphausiids).

In sum, planktonic invertebrate predators do not appear to be an important source of mortality for anchovy larvae other than during the yolk-sac stage. These predators may have an important effect on other fish larvae, however, but no adequate documentation exists. Squid, *Loligo opalescens*, might be an important predator of anchovy larvae; they co-occur with anchovy (Cailliet et al., 1979) and feed upon them, but *Euphausia* is their principal food (Karpov and Cailliet, 1978).

Fishes

Perhaps the most important group of predators of marine fish eggs and larvae are schooling pelagic juvenile and adult fishes. Analysis of stomach contents of such fishes usually indicates they do indeed eat larval fishes and eggs. It would be a formidable task to review this large literature, but I will cite a few examples for clupeoid fishes, the most important group of larval and egg predators because of their abundance, schooling behavior, and planktonic feeding habits.

Larval sand eel, *Ammodytes* (ca. 33 mm), comprise about 10% of the total food items eaten by North Sea herring in the Shields area from 1930 to 1934 (Savage, 1937) and about 42% of the food organisms eaten by herring from the southern North Sea and Tyne area (Hardy, 1924). Both authors cited found a variety of other fish eggs and larvae in herring stomachs as well, but at lower abundances. More recently, Pommeranz (in press) observed that at one station 54% of the wet weight of the stomach contents of herring and 45% of that of spratt (*Sprattus sprattus* L.) were composed of fish eggs and larvae. Average values for eggs in herring stomachs ranged from 0.03% to 51.1% (on the average, about 4 eggs per stomach) and the proportion of fish larvae from 0% to 3%. Harding et al. (1978) found that stomachs of herring taken in egg patches in the North Sea contained about 3% fish eggs and 62% fish larvae.

Feeding of the scombrid (*Rastrelliger kanagurta*) on the eggs of the labrid (*Thallusoma*) has been actively observed by Colin (1976). *Thallosoma* engaged in mass spawning which involved an upward rush and visible release of eggs and sperm; about five *Rastrelliger* converged on the site and began filter feeding on the eggs while swimming in tight circles.

My observations of the feeding behavior of northern anchovy are nearly identical to those of Colin (1976); when anchovy eggs were added to a tank, the school swam over the area and began filtering intensively while swimming in an elliptical orbit through the egg patch. Many reports exist for anchovy feeding on eggs and larvae of marine fishes including their own. In southern California, the most abundant pelagic planktivorous fish is the anchovy, hence they may be one of the major predators of fish eggs and larvae in the open sea. In a recent study (Hunter and Kimbrell, 1980b), stomach contents of anchovy taken during a peak spawning month contained on the average 5.1 anchovy eggs per fish. They used these data to calculate a daily ration of eggs of 86 eggs per fish and estimated that this represented about 17% of the eggs spawned per night, or about 32% of the daily mortality of eggs. They point out that the number of anchovy eggs in stomachs increased exponentially with the density of eggs in the sea, indicating that patchiness of eggs and selectivity of filtering by the schools probably play a major role in egg consumption. Very few larvae of any species occurred in the stomachs, but Hunter and Kimbrell's laboratory observations indicate that the smallest and most abundant anchovy larvae (3–5 mm SL) are digested beyond recognition in less than half an hour, whereas eggs are more resistant to digestion. Although no evidence exists, I believe that the younger larval stages are as vulnerable as eggs. Larvae probably remain highly vulnerable to schooling planktivorous fishes until avoidance abilities develop sufficiently. Yolk-sac larvae are readily eaten in the laboratory by anchovy, and their low incidence in field-caught specimens is probably the result of the rapid digestion rate and the decline in patchiness and abundance.

Conclusions

An understanding of the causes of larval mortality demands a thorough understanding of early life history traits. Traits discussed in these lectures include parental factors of time and place of spawning, pattern of spawn distribution, egg size and yolk reserves and such larval characters as feeding behavior, prey selection patterns, swimming and searching behavior, metabolism, growth rate, and time to the onset of schooling. These traits are interrelated and consequently form distinct life history strategies.

Food size preferences may be one of the better traits for identifying life history strategies. For example, to feed on a large prey requires a large mouth and a greater and more efficient effort because of the exponential decline in food density with food size. Persistence in attack and maneuverability would appear to be essential for a large prey strategy. Greater searching effort may require a faster swimming speed, and this in turn implies less vulnerability to predation and higher metabolic rate and energy requirements. The latter promotes faster growth (Kerr, 1971a, 1971b), and faster growth reduces the duration of the larval stage, the period of greatest vulnerability to predation, and the time to the onset of schooling. Mackerel and tunas appear to have adopted this large prey-fast growth strategy, whereas anchovy follow a small prey strategy. The sparid *Archosargus rhomboidalis*, which seems to fit in many respects the large prey feeding strategy, is affected much more by laboratory stocking density and is better able to take advantage of short-term patchiness of food than is the engraulid fish *Anchoa mitchilli* (Houde and Schekter, 1978). These tendencies are in keeping with the difference in searching power and efficiency of feeding implicit in large and small prey feeding strategies.

At high spawn densities, suppression of intraspecific effects on growth would be adaptive as well as suppression of sibling cannibalism. Species with slow cruising speeds, such as anchovy, might require higher initial larval densities to assure the socialization necessary for the onset of schooling or to form schools of viable size. Mackerel and tunas, on the other hand, are prone to sibling cannibalism and may not be affected by low spawning densities because the time to school formation is less, because growth is rapid and cruising speeds are higher, thus permitting more rapid formation of schools. Many other possible strategies exist other than those discussed for anchovy and scombroids. Species that hatch from large eggs in a relatively large and mature stage—flying fish, herring larvae, and saury, for example—have distinctly different life strategies.

My emphasis in these lectures on feeding ecology was on specific differences and how they form distinct life history strategies in the larval phase. The apparent similarities in feeding habits among pelagic larvae are striking nonetheless. Nearly all pelagic larvae are diurnal particulate planktivores, specializing in the young stages of copepods, whereas the feeding habits of the adults are much more diverse. Pelagic fish larvae are the most similar in the early stages of development, and distinctions become marked as development proceeds and larvae approach metamorphosis.

The literature I have reviewed on feeding ecology and on predation in larval fishes indicates that the smallest life stages are without doubt the most vulnerable to starvation and predation. Low feeding success, low resistance to starvation, and slow absolute swimming speeds all indicate that larvae are more vulnerable to starvation at the time of first feeding than at any other time. Similarly, the ability to avoid predation is dependent on burst speeds, the ability to sustain that speed, and the developmental state of sensory and locomotor systems. All of these improve rapidly with larval size or age. In addition, the number of potential predators may decrease with an increase in larval size; the highest number may occur during the yolk-sac period when larvae may be eaten by small planktonic invertebrates as well as by larger invertebrates and fishes.

Although the high early mortality of marine larvae is documented (May, 1974; Jones and Hall, 1974; Vladimirov, 1975), no conclusive evidence exists that variation in the rates of early mortality determines the strength of incoming year classes. This idea, Hjort's critical period concept (Hjort, 1914; May, 1974; Vladimirov, 1975), has long been postulated as a mechanism for variation in year class strength. It now appears, at least for the northern anchovy, that except for a few extreme cases it is not possible to detect changes in recruitment potential from the abundances of embryonic or postembryonic larvae up to 15 mm in length (Zweifel and Smith, in press). Thus identification of mechanisms regulating recruitment will probably require study of the entire larval and juvenile stages.

A recurrent theme in these lectures has been the role of patchiness in the early life history of fishes. Patchiness affects food availability which in turn may produce patchiness in larval survival and growth. Although direct links between food patches and survival have not been documented, the circumstantial evidence is strong. Larval food exists in patches (Lasker, 1975), and small-scale patchiness in growth and starvation exists (Methot and Kramer, 1979; O'Connell, 1981). Patchiness may also affect vulnerability to planktivorous predators, the onset of schooling behavior, and sibling cannibalism.

If patchiness controls larval survival, variation in recruitment ultimately may be the result of the summation of events occurring in a multitude of egg and larval patches. Although this increases the complexity of the problem, techniques now exist to study it. It is now possible to make reliable instantaneous estimates of the incidence of starvation (O'Connell, 1976, 1981; Theilacker, 1978) and of larval growth (Buckley, 1980; Methot, in press). Such estimates need to be related to the condition of the plankton community from which they were taken. Measures of community condition, such as standing crop of microcopepods, indices of naupliar production rate, primary production, oxygen, and nutrients, and other biotic and abiotic characteristics need to be related to instantaneous growth rates and starvation from the same patch. Such a dynamic description of the local community or patch condition could then be used to calibrate oceanic events in terms of larval growth and survival. In addition, these sets of dynamic descriptions and their larval correlates would provide the necessary data for a dynamic model of larval mortality.

Most of the work on the ecology of marine fish larvae has been laboratory studies on behavior and feeding ecology of the larvae produced by major offshore fish stocks. Little work has been done on the early life history of tropical reef fishes and many other inshore forms. Predation has received little attention in all species. Field studies on natural causes of mortality and variation of growth are just beginning, but the tools now exist for such work. If we are to identify the causes of natural mortality in the sea, the incidence of starvation and predation must be estimated over the spawning range of the species and at all life stages, and these losses compared with estimated rates of mortality. The vertical position of larvae in the sea in relation to their foods, predators, and time of day also needs to be considered in such an analysis.

References

Alvariño, A. 1980. The relation between the distribution of zooplankton predators and anchovy larvae. Calif. Coop. Oceanic Fish. Invest. Rep. 21:150–160.

Arthur, D.K. 1976. Food and feeding of larvae of three fishes occurring in the California Current, *Sardinops sagax*, *Engraulis mordax*, and *Trachurus symmetricus*. U.S. Fish. Bull. 74:517–530.

———. 1977. Distribution, size and abundance of microcopepods in the California Current system and their possible influence on survival of marine teleost larvae. U.S. Fish. Bull. 75:601–611.

Bagenal, T.B. 1971. The interrelation of the size of fish eggs, the date of spawning and the production cycle. J. Fish. Biol. 3:207–219.

Bainbridge, R. 1958. The speed of swimming of fish as related to size and to the frequency and amplitude of the tail beat. J. Exp. Biol. 35:109–133.

Beers, J.R., and G.L. Stewart. 1967. Micro-zooplankton in the euphotic zone at five locations across the California Current. J. Fish. Res. Bd. Canada 24:2053–2068.

———. 1970. Numerical abundance and estimated biomass of micro-zooplankton. *In* The Ecology of the Plankton off La Jolla, California, in the Period April through September, 1967 (Part VI), (ed. J.D.H. Strickland) Bull. Scripps Instn. Oceanog. 17:67–87.

———. 1971. Micro-zooplankters in the plankton communities of the upper waters of the eastern tropical Pacific. Deep Sea Res. 18:861–883.

Beukema, J.J. 1968. Predation by the three-spined stickleback (*Gasterosteus aculeatus* L.): the influence of hunger and experience. Behaviour 31:1–126.

Blaxter, J.H.S. 1965. The feeding of herring larvae and their ecology in relation to feeding. Calif. Coop. Oceanic Fish. Invest. Rep. 10:79–88.

———. 1968a. Visual thresholds and spectral sensitivity of herring larvae. J. Exp. Biol. 48:39–53.

———. 1968b. Light intensity, vision, and feeding in young plaice. J. Exp. Mar. Biol. Ecol. 2:293–307.

———. 1969. Development: eggs and larvae. *In* Fish Physiology, Vol. 3, (ed. W.S. Hoar and D.J. Randall), pp. 177–252, Academic Press, New York.

———. 1970. Light. *In* Marine Ecology, a Comprehensive, Integrated Treatise on Life in Oceans and Coastal Waters, vol. 1. *Environmental Factors*, (ed. O. Kinne), pp. 213–320, Wiley-Interscience, New York.

———. 1975. Reared and wild fish—how do they compare? *In* 10th European Symp. on Marine Biology, Ostend, Belgium, Sept. 17–23, 1975, pp. 11–26, Universa Press, Wetteren, Belgium.

Blaxter, J.H.S., and G. Hempel. 1963. The influence of egg size on herring larvae. J. Cons. Perm. int. Explor. Mer 28:211–240.

Blaxter, J.H.S., and M.E. Staines. 1971. Food searching potential in marine fish larvae. *In* 4th European Marine Biology Symp. (ed. D.J. Crisp), pp. 467–485. Cambridge Univ. Press, Cambridge.

Blaxter, J.H.S., and K.F. Ehrlich. 1974. Changes in behaviour during starvation of herring and plaice larvae. *In* The Early Life History of Fish, (ed. J.H.S. Blaxter), pp. 575–588, Springer-Verlag, Berlin.

Bowers, A.B., and D.I. Williamson. 1951. Food of larval and early post-larval stages of autumn-spawned herring in Manx waters. Annual Rep. Mar. Biol. Stat. Pt. Erin 63:17–26.

Braum, E. 1967. The survival of fish larvae with reference to their feeding behaviour and the food supply. *In* The Biological Basis of Freshwater Fish Production (ed. S.D. Gerking), pp. 113–131. Blackwell Scientific Publications, Oxford.

Breder, C.M., Jr., and L.A. Krumholz. 1943. On the locomotor and feeding behavior of certain postlarval Clupeoidea. Zoologica 28:61–67.

Breder, C.M., Jr., and F. Halpern. 1946. Innate and acquired behavior affecting the aggregation of fishes. Physiol. Zool. 19:154–190.

Buckley, L.J. 1980. Changes in ribonucleic acid, deoxyribonucleic acid and protein content during ontogenesis in winter flounder, *Pseudopleuronectes americanus*, and effect of starvation. U.S. Fish. Bull. 77:703–708.

Cailliet, G.M., K.A. Karpov, and D.A. Ambrose. 1979. Pelagic assemblages as determined from purse seine and large midwater trawl catches in Monterey Bay and their affinities with the market squid, *Loligo opalescens*. Calif. Coop. Oceanic Fish. Invest. Rep. 20:21–30.

Ciechomski, J.D. de, and G. Weiss. 1974. Estudios sobre la alimentacion de larvas de la merluza, *Merluccius merluccius* Hubbsi y de la anchoita, *Engraulis anchoita* en la mar. Physis. Secc. A. Buenos Aires 33:199–208.

Clemens, H.B. 1956. Rearing larval scombrid fishes in shipboard aquaria. Calif. Dept. Fish and Game 42:69–79.

Colin, P.L. 1976. Filter feeding and predation on the eggs of *Thallasoma* sp. by the scombroid fish *Rastrelliger kanagurta*. Copeia 1976:596–597.

Confer, J.L., and P.I. Blades. 1975. Omnivorous zooplankton and planktivorous fish. Limnol. Oceanogr. 20:571–579.

Curio, E. 1976. The Ethology of Predation. Springer-Verlag, Berlin, 250 pp.

Cushing, D.H., and J.G.K. Harris. 1973. Stock and recruitment and the problem of density dependence. Rapp. P.-v. Réun. Cons. Perm. int. Explor. Mer, 164:142–155.

Detwyler, R., and E.D. Houde. 1970. Food selection by laboratory-reared larvae of the scaled sardine *Harengula pensacolae* (Pisces, Clupeidae) and the bay anchovy *Anchoa mitchilli* (Pisces, Engraulidae). Mar. Biol. 7:214–222.

Duka, L.A. 1969. Feeding of larvae of the anchovy [*Engraulis encrasicholus maeoticus* Pusanov] in the Azov Sea. Probl. Ichthyol. 9:223–230 (transl. from Vop. Ikhtiol.).

Eaton, R.C., R.D. Farley, C.B. Kimmel, and E. Schabtach. 1977. Functional development in the Mauthner cell system of embryos and larvae of the zebra fish. J. Neurobiol. 8:151–172.

Feigenbaum, D., and M.R. Reeve. 1977. Prey detection in the Chaetognatha: response to a vibrating probe and experimental determination of attack distance in large aquaria. Limnol. Oceanogr. 22:1052–1058.

Frazer, J.H. 1969. Experimental feeding of some medusae and Chaetognatha. J. Fish. Res. Bd. Canada 26:1743–1762.

Gorbunova, N.N., and N. Ya. Lipskaya. 1975. Feeding of larvae of the blue marlin *Makaira nigricans* (Pisces, Istiophoridae). J. Ichthyol. 15: 95–101 (transl. from Vopr. Ikhtiol.).

Gruzov, L.N., and L.G. Alekseyeva. 1970. Weight characteristics of copepods from the equatorial Atlantic. Oceanology 10:871–879 (transl. from Okeanologiya).

Harding, D., J.H. Nichols, and D.S. Tungate. 1978. The spawning of plaice (*Pleuronectes platessa* L.) in the southern North Sea and English Channel. *In* North Sea Fish Stocks—Recent Changes and Their Causes (ed. G. Hempel), Rapp. P.-v. Réun. Cons. Perm. int. Explor. Mer 172:102–113.

Hardy, A.C. 1924. The herring in relation to its animate environment. Part I. The food and feeding habits of the herring with special reference to the east coast of England. Fish. Invest. London 7:1–53.

Helfrich, P., and P.M. Allen. 1975. Observations on the spawning of mullet, *Crenimugil crenilabis* (Forskål), at Enewetak, Marshall Islands. Micronesia 11:219–225.

Hjort, J. 1914. Fluctuations in the great fisheries of northern Europe viewed in the light of biological research. Rapp. P.-v. Réun. Cons. Perm. int. Explor. Mer 20:1–228.

Hobson, E.S., and J.R. Chess. 1978. Tropical relationships among fishes and plankton in the lagoon at Enewetak Atoll, Marshall Islands. U.S. Fish. Bull. 76:133–153.

Holling, C.S. 1966. The functional response of invertebrate predators to prey density. Mem. Entomol. Soc. Canada 48:1–86.

Houde, E.D. 1972. Development and early life history of the northern sennet, *Sphyraena borealis* DeKay (Pisces: Sphyraenidae) reared in the laboratory. U.S. Fish. Bull. 70:185–195.

———. 1973. Some recent advances and unsolved problems in the culture of marine fish larvae. Proc. Wld. Maricult. Soc. 3:83–112.

———. 1974. Effects of temperature and delayed feeding on growth and survival of larvae of three species of subtropical marine fishes. Mar. Biol. 26:271–285.

———. 1975. Effects of stocking density and food density on survival, growth and yield of laboratory-reared larvae of sea bream *Archosargus rhomboidalis* (L.) (Sparidae). J. Fish. Biol. 7:115–127.

———. 1977. Food concentrations and stocking density effects on survival and growth of laboratory-reared larvae of bay anchovy *Anchoa mitchilli* and lined sole *Achirus lineatus*. Mar. Biol. 43:333–341.

———. 1978. Critical food concentrations for larvae of three species of subtropical marine fishes. Bull. Mar. Sci. 28:395–411.

Houde, E.D., and R. Schekter. 1978. Simulated food patches and survival of larval bay anchovy, *Anchoa mitchilli*, and sea bream, *Archosargus rhomboidalis*. U.S. Fish. Bull. 76:483–486.

Howell, B.R. 1973. Marine fish culture in Britain. VIII. A marine rotifer, *Brachionus plicatilis* Muller, and the larvae of the mussel, *Mytilus edulis* L., as foods for larval flatfish. J. Cons. int. Explor. Mer 35:1–6.

Hunter, J.R. 1972. Swimming and feeding behavior of larval anchovy, *Engraulis mordax*. U.S. Fish. Bull. 70:821–838.

———. 1976. Culture and growth of northern anchovy, *Engraulis mordax*, larvae. U.S. Fish. Bull. 74:81–88.

———. 1977. Behavior and survival of northern anchovy *Engraulis mordax* larvae. Calif. Coop. Oceanic Fish. Invest. Rep. 19:138–146.

———. 1981. The feeding ecology of marine fish larvae. *In* Fish Behavior and Its Use in the Capture and Culture of Fishes (eds. J.E. Bardach, J.J. Magnuson, R.C. May, and J. M. Reinhart), ICLARM Conf. Proc. 5, Interntl. Center for Living Aquatic Resources Mgmt., Manila. p. 287–330.

Hunter, J.R., and J.R. Zweifel. 1971. Swimming speed, tail beat frequency, tail beat amplitude and size in jack mackerel, *Trachurus symmetricus*, and other fishes. U.S. Fish. Bull. 69:253–266.

Hunter, J.R., and G.L. Thomas. 1974. Effect of prey distribution and density on the searching and feeding behavior of larval anchovy *Engraulis mordax* Girard, pp. 559–574. *In* The Early Life History of Fish, (ed. J.H.S. Blaxter), Springer-Verlag, Berlin.

Hunter, J.R., and C. Sanchez. 1976. Diel changes in swim bladder inflation of the larvae of the northern anchovy, *Engraulis mordax*. U.S. Fish. Bull. 74:847–855.

Hunter, J.R., and S.R. Goldberg. 1980. Spawning incidence and batch fecundity in northern anchovy, *Engraulis mordax*. U.S. Fish. Bull. 77:641–652.

Hunter, J.R., and B.J. Macewicz. 1980. Sexual maturity, batch fecundity, spawning frequency, and temporal pattern of spawning for the northern anchovy, *Engraulis mordax*, during the 1979 spawning season. Calif. Coop. Oceanic Fish. Invest. Rept. 21:139–149.

Hunter, J.R., and C.A. Kimbrell. 1980a. Early life history of Pacific mackerel, *Scomber japonicus*. U.S. Fish. Bull. 78:89–101.

Hunter, J.R., and C.A. Kimbrell. 1980b. Egg cannibalism in the northern anchovy, *Engraulis mordax*. U.S. Fish. Bull. 78:811–816.

Ivlev, V.S. 1960. On the utilization of food by planktophage fishes. Bull. Math. Biophysics 22:371–389.

————. 1961. Experimental Ecology of the Feeding of Fishes, 302 pp. Yale Univ. Press, New Haven.

Johannes, R.E. 1978. Reproductive strategies of coastal marine fishes in the tropics. Env. Biol. Fish. 3:65–84.

Jones, R., and W.B. Hall. 1974. Some observations on the population dynamics of the larval stage in the common gadoids, *In* The Early Life History of Fish (ed. J.H.S. Blaxter) pp. 87–102, Springer-Verlag, Berlin.

Karpov, K.A., and G.M. Cailliet. 1978. Feeding dynamics of *Loligo opalescens*, pp. 45–65. *In* Biological, Oceanographic, and Acoustic Aspects of the market Squid, *Loligo opalescens* Berry, (ed. C.W. Recksiek and H.W. Frey). Calif. Dept. Fish and Game, Fish Bull. 169.

Kerr, S.R. 1971a. Analysis of laboratory experiments on growth efficiency of fishes. J. Fish. Res. Bd. Canada 28:801–808.

————. 1971b. Prediction of fish growth efficiency in nature. J. Fish. Res. Bd. Canada 28:809–814.

Kislalioglu, M., and R.N. Gibson. 1976a. Some factors governing prey selection by the 15-spined stickleback, *Spinachia spinachia* (L.). J. Exp. Mar. Biol. Ecol. 25:159–169.

————. 1976b. Prey 'handling time' and its importance in food selection by the 15-spined stickleback, *Spinachia spinachia* (L.). J. Exp. Mar. Biol. Ecol. 25:151–158.

Kleerekoper, H., A.M. Timms, G.F. Westlake, F.B. Davy, T. Malar, and V.M. Anderson. 1970. An analysis of locomotor behaviour of goldfish *(Carassius auratus)*. Anim. Behav. 18:317–330.

Kuhlmann, D. 1977. Laboratory studies on the feeding behaviour of the chaetognaths *Sagitta setosa* J. Müller and *S. elegans* Verril with special reference to fish eggs and larvae as food organisms. Sonderdruck aus Bd. 25:163–171.

Lasker, R. 1975. Field criteria for survival of anchovy larvae: the relation between inshore chlorophyll maximum layers and successful first feeding. U.S. Fish. Bull. 73:453–462.

Lasker, R., H.M. Feder, G.H. Theilacker, and R.C. May. 1970. Feeding, growth and survival of *Engraulis mordax* larvae reared in the laboratory. Mar. Biol. 5:345–353.

Laurence, G.C. 1972. Comparative swimming abilities of fed and starved larval largemouth bass *(Micropterus salmoides)*. J. Fish Biol. 4:73–78.

————. 1974. Growth and survival of haddock *(Melanogrammus aeglefinus)* larvae in relation to planktonic prey concentration. J. Fish. Res. Bd. Canada 31: 1415–1419.

————. 1975. Laboratory growth and metabolism of the winter flounder *Pseudopleuronectes americanus* from hatching through metamorphosis at three temperatures. Mar. Biol. 32:223–229.

Laurence, G.C., and C.A. Rogers. 1976. Effects of temperature and salinity on comparative embryo development and mortality of Atlantic cod (*Gadus morhua* L.) and haddock (*Melanogrammus aeglefinus* (L.). J. Cons. int. Explor. Mer. 36:220–228.

Lebour, M.V. 1921. The food of young clupeoids. J. Mar. Biol. Assoc. U.K. 12:458–467.

————. 1922. The food of plankton organisms. J. Mar. Biol. Assoc. U.K. 12:644–677.

————. 1923. The food of plankton organisms, II. J. Mar. Biol. Assoc. U.K. 13:70–92.

————. 1925. Young anglers in captivity and some of their enemies. J. Mar. Biol. Assoc. U.K. 13:721–734.

Lenarz, W.H. 1973. Dependence of catch rates on size of fish larvae. Rapp. P.-v. Réun. Con. int. Explor. Mer 164:270–275.

Lillelund, K., and R. Lasker. 1971. Laboratory studies on predation by marine copepods on fish larvae. U.S. Fish. Bull. 69:655–667.

Lloyd, M. 1967. "Mean crowding." J. Anim. Ecol. 36:1–30.

Lovegrove, T. 1966. The determination of the dry weight of plankton and the effect of various factors on the values obtained, *In* Some Contemporary Studies in Marine Science, (ed. H. Barnes), pp. 429–467. Hafner Publ. Co., New York.

Marshall, S.M., and A.P. Orr. 1955. The Biology of a Marine Copepod *Calanus finmarchicus* (Gunnerus), 188 pp., Oliver & Boyd, Edinburgh.

Matsuura, Y. 1977. A study of the life history of the Brazilian sardine, *Sardinella brasiliensis*. IV. Distribution and abundance of sardine larvae. Bolm. Inst. Oceanogr., São Paulo, 26:219–247.

May, R.C. 1970. Feeding larval marine fishes in the laboratory: a review. Calif. Coop. Oceanic Fish. Invest. Rep. 14:76–83.

———. 1971. Effects of delayed initial feeding on larvae of the grunion, *Leuresthes tenuis* (Ayres). U.S. Fish. Bull. 69:411–425.

———. 1974. Larval mortality in marine fishes and the critical period concept, *In* The Early Life History of Fish (ed. J.H.S. Blaxter), pp. 3–19. Springer-Verlag, New York.

Mayo, C.A. 1973. Rearing, growth and development of the eggs and larvae of seven scombrid fishes from the Straits of Florida. Ph.D. dissertation, Univ. Miami, 127 pp.

Methot, R.D. In press. Spatial covariation of daily growth rates of larval northern anchovy, *Engraulis mordax*, and northern lampfish, *Stenobrachius leucopsarus*. ICES Symp. on Early Life History of Fish, Woods Hole, Mass., April 1979. Rapp. P.-v. Réun. Cons. int. Explor. Mer 178.

Methot, R.D., and D. Kramer. 1979. Growth of northern anchovy, *Engraulis mordax*, larvae in the sea. U.S. Fish. Bull. 77:413–423.

Mikhman, A.S. 1969. Some new data on the larval feeding of the Azov tyul'ka [*Clupeonella delicatula* (Nordm.)] and on the role of the nutritional factor in fluctuations in its abundance. Probl. Ichthyol. 9:666–673 (transl. from Vop. Ikhtiol.).

Murphy, G.I., and R.I. Clutter. 1972. Sampling anchovy larvae with a plankton purse seine. U.S. Fish. Bull. 70:789–798.

O'Connell, C.P. 1976. Histological criteria for diagnosing the starving condition in early post yolk-sac larvae of the northern anchovy, *Engraulis mordax* Girard. J. Exp. Mar. Biol. Ecol. 25:285–312.

———. 1980. Percentage of starving northern anchovy, *Engraulis mordax*, larvae in the sea as estimated by histological methods. U.S. Fish. Bull. 78:475–489.

———. 1981. Development of organ systems in the northern anchovy, *Engraulis mordax*, and other teleosts. Am. Zool. 21:429–446.

O'Connell, C.P., and L.P. Raymond. 1970. The effect of food density on survival and growth of early post yolk-sac larvae of the northern anchovy (*Engraulis mordax* Girard) in the laboratory. J. Exp. Mar. Biol. Ecol. 5:187–197.

Paffenhöfer, G.-A. 1971. Grazing and ingestion rates of nauplii, copepodids and adults of the marine planktonic copepod, *Calanus helgolandicus*. Mar. Biol. 11:286–298.

Pommeranz, T. In press. Observations on the predation of herring (*Clupea harengus* L.) and sprat (*Sprattus sprattus* L.) on fish eggs and larvae in the southern North Sea. ICES Symp. on Early Life History of Fish, Woods Hole, Mass., April 1979. Rapp. P.-v. Réun. Cons. int. Explor. Mer 178.

Qasim, S.Z. 1959. Laboratory experiments on some factors affecting the survival of marine teleost larvae. J. Mar. Biol. Assoc. India 1:13–25.

Riley, J.D. 1966. Marine fish culture in Britain VII. Plaice (*Pleuronectes platessa* L.) post-larval feeding on *Artemia salina* L. nauplii and the effects of varying feeding levels. J. Cons. Perm. int. Explor. Mer 30:204–221.

———. 1974. The distribution and mortality of sole eggs [*Solea solea* (L.)] in inshore areas, *In* The Early Life History of Fish, (ed. J.H.S. Blaxter), pp. 39–52. Springer-Verlag, Berlin.

Rojas de Mendiola, B. 1974. Food of the larval anchoveta *Engraulis ringens* J. *In* The Early Life History of Fish, (ed. J.H.S. Blaxter), pp. 277–285. Springer-Verlag, New York.

Rosenthal, H., and G. Hempel. 1970. Experimental studies in feeding and food requirements of herring larvae (*Clupea harengus* L.) *In* Marine Food Chains (ed. J.H.S. Steele), pp. 344–364. Univ. Calif. Press, Berkeley.

Rosenthal, H., and M. Fonds. 1973. Biological observations during rearing experiments with the garfish *Belone belone*. Mar. Biol. 21:203–218.

Ryland, J.S., and J.H. Nichols. 1967. Effect of temperature on the efficiency of growth of plaice prolarvae. Nature 214:529–530.

Savage, R.E. 1937. The food of North Sea herring, 1930–1934. Fish. Invest. London 15:1–57.

Scura, E.D., and C.W. Jerde. 1977. Various species of phytoplankton as food for larval northern anchovy, *Engraulis mordax*, and relative nutritional value of the dinoflagellates *Gymnodinium splendens* and *Gonyaulax polydera*. U.S. Fish. Bull. 75:577–583.

Sette, O.E. 1943. Biology of the Atlantic mackerel (*Scomber scombrus*) of North America. Part I. Early life history, including the growth, drift, and mortality of the egg and larval populations. U.S. Fish. Wildl. Serv. Fish Bull. 50:148–237.

Shaw, E. 1961. The development of schooling behavior in fishes. Physiol. Zool. 34:263–272.

Sheader, M., and F. Evans. 1975. Feeding and gut structure of *Parathemisto gaudichaudi* (Guerin) (Amphipoda, Hyperiidea). J. Mar. Biol. Assoc. U.K. 55:641–656.

Shelbourne, J.E. 1962. A predator-prey size relationship for plaice larvae feeding on *Oikopleura*. J. Mar. Biol. Assoc. U.K. 42:243–252.

Sheldon, R.W., and T.R. Parsons. 1967. A continuous size spectrum for particulate matter in the sea. J. Fish. Res. Bd. Canada 24:909–915.

Sheldon, R.W., A. Prakash, and W.H. Sutcliffe, Jr. 1972. The size distribution of particles in the ocean. Limnol. Oceanogr. 17:327–340.

Shirota, A. 1970. Studies on the mouth size of fish larvae. (In Jap. Engl. summary.) Bull. Jap. Soc. Sci. Fish. 36:353–368. (Transl. by Fish. Res. Bd. Canada Transl. Ser. 1978.)

Smith, P.E. 1973. The mortality and dispersal of sardine eggs and larvae. Rapp. R.-v. Réun. Cons. Perm. int. Explor. Mer 164:282–292.

Stepien, W.P., Jr. 1976. Feeding of laboratory-reared larvae of the sea bream *Archosargus rhomboidalis* (Sparidae). Mar. Biol. 38:1–16.

Theilacker, G.H. 1978. Effect of starvation on the histological and morphological characteristics of jack mackerel, *Trachurus symmetricus*, larvae. U.S. Fish. Bull. 76:403–414.

Theilacker, G.H., and M.F. McMaster. 1971. Mass culture of the rotifer *Brachionus plicatilis* and its evaluation as a food for larval anchovies. Mar. Biol. 10:183–188.

Theilacker, G.H., and R. Lasker. 1974. Laboratory studies of predation by Euphausiid shrimps on fish larvae *In* The Early Life History of Fish, (ed. J.H.S. Blaxter), pp. 287–299. Springer-Verlag, Berlin.

Thines, G., and E. Vandenbussche. 1966. The effects of alarm substance on the schooling behavior of *Rasbora heteromorpha* Duncker in day and night conditions. Anim. Behav. 14:296–302.

Vladimirov, V.I. 1975. Critical periods in the development of fishes. J. Ichthyol. 15:851–868 (transl. from Vopr. Ikhtiol.).

Vlymen, W.J., III. 1974. Swimming energetics of the larval anchovy, *Engraulis mordax*. U.S. Fish. Bull. 72:885–899.

———. 1977. A mathematical model of the relationship between larval anchovy (*Engraulis mordax*) growth, prey microdistribution, and larval behavior. Environ. Biol. Fishes 2:211–233.

Ware, D.M. 1975. Relation between egg size, growth, and natural mortality of larval fish. J. Fish. Res. Bd. Canada 32:2503–2512.

Webb, P.W. 1978. Hydrodynamics: nonscombrid fish. *In* Fish Physiology, Vol. 7 (ed. W.S. Hoar and D.J. Randall), pp. 189–237, Academic Press, New York.

Weihs, D. 1980. Energetic significance of changes in swimming modes during growth of larval anchovy, *Engraulis mordax*. U.S. Fish. Bull. 77:597–604.

Westernhagen, H. von. 1976. Some aspects of the biology of the hyeriid amphipod *Hyperoche medusarum.* Helgölander wiss. Meeresunters. 28: 43–50.

Westernhagen, H. von, and H. Rosenthal. 1976. Predator-prey relationship between Pacific herring, *Clupea harengus* Pallasi, larvae and a predatory hyperiid amphipod, *Hyperoche medusarum.* U.S. Fish. Bull. 74:669–674.

Wiborg, K.F. 1948a. Experiments with the Clarke-Bumpus plankton sampler and with a plankton pump in the Lofoten area in northern Norway. Fiskeridir. Skr. Havundersøk. 9(2), 32 pp.

———. 1948b. Investigations on cod larvae in the coastal waters of northern Norway. Fiskeridir. Skr. Havunderso/k. 9(3), 27 pp.

Wyatt, T. 1972. Some effects of food density on the growth and behaviour of plaice larvae. Mar. Biol. 14:210–216.

Yokota, T., M. Toriyama, F. Kanai, and S. Nomura. 1961. Studies on the feeding habit of fishes. (In Jap., Engl. summary.) Rep. Nankai Reg. Fish. Res. Lab. 14, 234 pp.

Zweifel, J.R., and P.E. Smith. In press. Estimates of abundance and mortality of larval anchovies (1951–1975): application of a new method. ICES Symp. on Early Life History of Fish, Woods Hole, Mass., April 1979. Rapp. P.-v. Réun. Cons. int. Explor. Mer 178.

The Role of a Stable Ocean in Larval Fish Survival and Subsequent Recruitment

Reuben Lasker

The Role of a Stable Ocean in Larval Fish Survival and Subsequent Recruitment

Pelagic fish populations can and do undergo precipitous and catastrophic recruitment failures. Peru suffered a massive collapse of its fishery for anchoveta, *Engraulis ringens* (Valdivia, 1978), resulting in a reduced catch from 1971 to 1973, i.e., from 12 million to 2 million tons, an economic disaster. Experts called in by the Food and Agriculture Organization of the United Nations and the government of Peru noted that the decline in the population of the Peruvian anchoveta had much in common with similar declines of other clupeoid species, e.g., the Atlanto-Scandian herring, the Pacific sardine, the Hokkaido herring, and the Japanese sardine (Murphy, 1974). They concluded that heavy fishing on a parent stock after the appearance of several poor year classes is sufficient to reduce the stock's reproductive potential to a point where it can no longer produce enough recruits for the fishery.

However, a very small population size did not prevent the recent resurgence in the fishery for the Japanese sardine, *Sardinops melanosticta*. This is a striking example of how a pelagic fish population can undergo a remarkable recruitment success. From 1964 to 1972, the Japanese sardine was virtually absent from local waters around Japan, but within five years (1973–1978) this fish increased steadily in numbers and now appears as a very large population around the home islands, particularly in local waters east of Honshu. The catch increased from a negligible one of a few thousand tons in 1972 to almost 1.64 million tons in 1978 (Fig. 1). Kondo (1980) attributed this increased catch to a single large year class which appeared *de novo* in 1972 and whose subsequent spawning successes from 1974 through 1977 provided the large tonnage of sardines to the fishery. Kondo believes that the breakdown of a long-established cold water cell adjacent to the coast permitted the Kuroshio Current to approach close to the home islands of Japan, that this led to an increase in the quantity of food available for larval fish (chiefly copepod nauplii), and resulted in enhanced larval survival with a subsequent increase in the sardine population.

The causes of natural large population changes cannot consistently be shown to be density dependent. The Japanese sardine is a good example of this. Its resurgence from extremely low population levels to one supporting a two-million-ton fishery in just a few years highlights anew the questions asked by fishery scientists: "To what extent can a pelagic stock be fished before subsequent year classes resulting from that stock are affected?" "At what

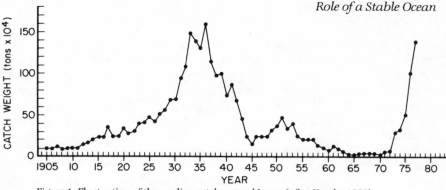

Figure 1. Fluctuation of the sardine catch around Japan (after Kondo, 1980).

population size of a fish can recruitment, the successful survival of fish from hatching to a size exploitable by a fishery, be shown to be density dependent, if at all?" Answers to these questions would help greatly in elucidating the relationship between stock and recruitment and ultimately the management of highly volatile pelagic stocks.

Over the past three decades, scientists have tried to find correlative physical, chemical, and biological ocean parameters which could be used to predict migration patterns, recruitment, and large fluctuations in population biomass—but with very limited success. The management of fish populations has marched apace, with decisions usually based on historical precedents but rarely on scientific principles. Yet the collapses of recruitment-limited fish populations have had enormous economic and social effects on fishing nations. These might have been avoided had there been reasonable predictions on the fate of the fish populations due to fishing and the environment.

The vastness of the ocean and the difficulty of sampling spatially and temporally present major problems to fisheries scientists. Fisheries managers would like useful "real time" information, but it is not uncommon to have to wait a year or longer to obtain data, process them, and reduce them to an interpretable form. Long delays in assessing the strength of incoming year classes introduce great uncertainties about future recruitment. Furthermore, most clupeoids recruit into the fishery from one to two years after they are born, accounting for a built-in delay. Statistics on cohorts, age, growth, and relative mortality must wait at least for the fish to grow up and be caught by the fishery. Predictions based on catch statistics are frequently too late to be useful, and the mechanisms determining the amount of future recruitment are not elucidated at all by a study of the catch.

Johan Hjort's Hypothesis of the Larval Fish Critical Period

While there have been a number of suggestions for investigating the stock and recruitment problem, in recent years scientists have tended toward the belief that vulnerable early life stages of pelagic fish hold some important

81

clues to understanding large variations in recruitment. This idea is not new. In 1914 the eminent Norwegian fishery biologist, Johan Hjort, suggested that year classes of the Atlanto-Scandian herring, *Clupea harengus,* fluctuate in magnitude according to the availability of food to its very earliest larval stages. He hypothesized that resultant year classes are small when food is scarce and large when food is abundant. Although Hjort had no direct measurements to support his idea, scientists find it attractive even today, although supporting evidence is still mostly inferential and speculative. After a 60-year hiatus, Hjort's idea has been resurrected and elaborated upon, and evidence has been and is being accumulated from the ocean and the laboratory to test its basic tenets.

Does a Good Year Class Depend on a Stable Ocean and Good Food?

In California at the National Marine Fisheries Service, Southwest Fisheries Center (SWFC), La Jolla, Lasker and his coworkers have developed an extension of the Hjort hypothesis which accepts the initial premise that food for first-feeding larvae may be limited but suggests that there are times and places in the sea where food aggregation occurs and that survival of larvae depends on these. Lasker (1975) describes the use of laboratory-produced first-feeding anchovy larvae to detect good feeding areas in the sea and to establish the threshold concentrations for feeding by the larva. The importance of a stable environment for feeding was demonstrated in these experiments, and at the time of this study the nearshore less-turbulent environment was shown to be better for larval anchovy feeding than offshore in the mainstream of the California Current. Cruises in late 1974 and 1975 (Lasker, 1978) revealed a 300-kilometer-long by 4-kilometer-wide patch of the thecate dinoflagellate, *Gonyaulax polyedra,* along the southern California coast in December and its extension to 40 kilometers wide in January. While present in concentrations above the threshold for feeding during these two months, *G. polyedra* also was demonstrated to be a poor food for anchovy larvae (Scura and Jerde, 1977). A massive upwelling along the coast in February 1975 wiped out the patch and reduced particle concentrations far below threshold-for-feeding by first-feeding anchovy larvae.

In addition to food density, survival of fish larvae also depends on particle size and species composition of food organisms (Lasker et al., 1970; Scura and Jerde, 1977). For instance, in March–April 1974 the naked dinoflagellate *Gymnodinium splendens* was the dominant food particle in the larva's environment and was known to be nutritious and desirable (Lasker et al., 1970). Thus species succession, particularly after upwelling periods, may result in the replacement of desirable food organisms (e.g., some species of dinoflagellates) with undesirable ones (e.g., diatoms), once again resulting in poor larval feeding conditions despite the fact that primary production may be high.

The 1975 spawning season of the northern anchovy can be summed up as follows: (1) *Gonyaulax polyedra*, a thecate dinoflagellate but a very poor food, dominated the first-feeding larva's environment; (2) an upwelling occurred late in the spawning season which swept out this poor food, but no suitable food appeared in its place; (3) 1975 produced one of the worst northern anchovy year classes on record.

To test these ideas further, Lasker and Zweifel (1978) produced a simulation model, based on laboratory and field data, of survival and growth of first-day-of-feeding anchovy larvae, *Engraulis mordax*, on different prey sizes and concentrations. They showed that at nominal capture efficiencies of 20–30 percent, there is a threshold of 30–50 small particles (45–55 μm diameter) per milliliter needed for substantial survival and growth. Large particles, e.g., copepod nauplii (95–105 μm diameter), can enhance survival when they are in concentrations of between 10 and 100 per liter, but the same environment must contain above-threshold numbers of small particles. This simulation showed an important distinction between survival and average growth; i.e., larvae may survive in significant numbers in feeding regimes in which the *average* growth for the population is negative. The concept relating larval fish food aggregation to stability of the water column and its relation to oceanographic and meteorological conditions needs to be tested in a variety of habitats.

Vlymen (1977) showed the importance of the geometry of prey distribution in his study of the larval anchovy in physical relation to its food. In particular, his simulation model indicated that extremely different larval anchovy growth rates in the sea are the most likely functions of prey contagion, with the highest growth rates not necessarily occurring at the highest level of prey contagion. Owen (in press) sampled within chlorophyll maximum layers on a vertical scale only 20 cm apart and found significant differences in numbers of potential larval fish food organisms, often between adjacent 20 cm water samples. This seems to confirm Vlymen's contention that the centimeter scale of aggregation must exist in the sea and that it occurs for every food type yet identified as needed for larval anchovy growth and survival.

Larval fish drift and the conditions which cause it are further elaborations of the Hjort hypothesis. Some scientists believe that upwelling events, if strong enough, can carry fish larvae out of good feeding areas into poor ones. At the California coast, when upwelling is weak, the stable environment inshore results in good feeding for young fish and enhanced survival. Working with fishery statistics on Pacific mackerel (*Scomber japonicus*) year-class strength, an upwelling index (Bakun, 1973), and a wind curl index (Bakun and Nelson, 1977), Parrish (1976) and Parrish and MacCall (1978) have shown good correlations of upwelling, surface transport patterns, and year-class strength of Pacific mackerel off California.

On the east coast of the United States, Nelson et al. (1977) showed that menhaden larvae, which depend on estuaries for food, are carried into estuaries during downwelling periods. In this case, upwelling acts to the detriment of larval survival by keeping larvae offshore, a mechanism different from the disruption of food aggregations shown to be important for northern anchovy larvae.

Storms also were found to disrupt larval food aggregations, and it has been inferred that this probably results in heavy larval mortality during the anchovy spawning season (Lasker, 1975). A regional cube-of-the-wind-speed index for the anchovy spawning grounds off California has been developed by Andrew Bakun at the Pacific Environmental Group (SWFC) of the National Marine Fisheries Service and used by Lasker (in press) to correlate with good and poor anchovy year classes.

While the data are still sparse, indications are that an index of this kind, which reflects the amount of mechanical energy available for stirring the upper layers of the ocean (Niiler and Krause, 1977), may be a valuable predictor of poor feeding conditions of larvae and hence the degree of recruitment. For example, a violent mid-December 1977 storm in southern California destroyed layers of potential larval anchovy food; stability was not restored to the upper layers of the inshore anchovy spawning region until March. Lasker, at the 1978 CalCOFI Conference, suggested that unusual storm conditions during winter 1977–78 would adversely affect the 1978 anchovy year class. Results of otolith birthdate analysis of recruits from the 1978 year class by Methot (quoted in Lasker, in press) bear this out; recruits were born mainly in March and April 1978, despite extensive spawning in December 1977 through February 1978.

Walsh et al. (1980) also provide evidence from Peru that confirms the idea that strong winds and turbulent seas can be detrimental to the survival of the Peruvian anchovy. On the other hand, Ware et al. (in press) suggest that aggregations of food for Peruvian anchovy larvae may be a *result* of strong winds by the production of Langmuir cells and consequent accumulation of likely food items in "windrows." The space and time scales of the events being considered differ greatly, and reconciliation of these ideas requires additional research into the effects of wind-mixing and the distribution of larval fish food particles.

The findings that anchovy larvae cannot feed on filamentous diatoms (Lasker, 1975, 1978), that only certain food organisms of the right size for feeding are nutritious (Lasker et al., 1970; Scura and Jerde, 1977), and that there is a low probability of the larva encountering copepod nauplii at first feeding (Lasker and Zweifel, 1978) have provided the biological framework with which to predict the quality of the ocean environment for survival of early anchovy larvae. Similar data are needed for other pelagic fish larvae, and studies have begun on a number of commercially important species to test the ideas suggested here (Ellertsen et al., in press).

Predation on Larval Fishes: An Unknown Factor

Predators on marine fish larvae usually are not discussed very much in relation to recruitment, despite the possibility that they may have great effects on larval survival and year class formation. Studies in the laboratory and in the sea have been more qualitative than quantitative. Exceptions to this rule are the recent studies of Hunter and Kimbrell (1980), who demonstrated that anchovy adults can be voracious predators on their own eggs and larvae, and the work of Lillelund and Lasker (1971), who pointed to the possibility that many pelagic copepods co-existing with fish larvae can bite and lethally damage them. Theilacker and Lasker (1974) also implicated euphausiids as potential predators of larval anchovies. Some fish larvae, such as those of the Pacific mackerel, are piscivorous and, in the laboratory at least, are known to eat their siblings (Hunter, this volume). Alvariño (1980), in an interesting investigation of the distribution of larvae, interpreted the inverse relation of patches of potential predators to patches of anchovy eggs and larvae as an evolutionary development in spawning behavior favoring survival of larvae.

Most of the information concerning predation on larval fishes is too sparse and unquantifiable. A great deal of work needs to be done in this area of study and requires a combination of laboratory and field observations before we will be able to assess the role of predation in recruitment processes.

Conclusion

While the bulk of the recruitment research described here has been on clupeoid fishes, the concepts advanced may be applicable to a wide variety of fishes having planktonic larvae. Minimum concentrations of food must be present in the larva's environment with associated stable ocean conditions to insure that threshold-for-feeding concentrations are maintained. Cube-of-the-wind-speed, upwelling, and wind curl indexes are new tools which can be used by fishery scientists to correlate with larval mortality, larval food distributions, and subsequent year-class strength. Biological information on larval fishes obtained in the laboratory now has even greater meaning since it can be used to erect useful predictive models of recruitment and, with specific data on the ocean environment, provides a hope for meaningful fishery prediction. If managers want to respond before there are sudden collapses or substantial increases in fish populations, it seems clear that they must take into consideration the increasing evidence that environmental factors have major effects on the survival of larval fish and that density-independent factors may be more important than previously believed.

References

Alvariño, A. (1980). The relation between the distribution of zooplankton predators and anchovy larvae. Calif. Coop. Oceanic Fish. Invest. Rep. 21:150–160.

Bakun, A. 1973. Coastal upwelling indices, west coast of North America, 1946–1971. U.S. Dept. Comm., NOAA Tech. Rept. NMFS SSRF-671, 103 pp.

Bakun, A., and C.S. Nelson. 1977. Climatology of upwelling related processes off Baja California. Calif. Coop. Oceanic Fish. Invest. Rep. 19:107–127.

Ellertsen, B., P. Solemdal, S. Sundby, S. Tilseth, T. Westgard, and V. Øiestad. In press. Feeding and vertical distribution of cod larvae in relation to availability of prey organisms. ICES Symp. on the Early Life History of Fish, Woods Hole, Mass., April 1979. Rapp. P.-v. Réun. Cons. int. Explor. Mer 178.

Hjort, J. 1914. Fluctuations in the great fisheries of northern Europe viewed in the light of biological research. Rapp. P.-v. Réun. Cons. Perm. int. Explor. Mer 20:1–228.

Hunter, J.R., and C. Kimbrell. 1980. Egg cannibalism in the northern anchovy, *Engraulis mordax*. U.S. Fish. Bull. 78:811–816.

Kondo, Keiichi. The recovery of the Japanese Sardine—the biological basis of stock-size fluctuations. Rapp. p.-v. Réun. Cons. int. Explor. Mer. 177:322-354.

Lasker, R. 1975. Field criteria for survival of anchovy larvae: the relation between inshore chlorophyll maximum layers and successful first feeding. U.S. Fish. Bull. 73:453–462.

———. 1978. The relation between oceanographic conditions and larval anchovy food in the California Current: identification of factors contributing to recruitment failure. Rapp. P.-v. Réun. Cons. int. Explor. Mer 173:212–230.

———. In press. Factors contributing to variable recruitment of the northern anchovy (*Engraulis mordax*) in the California Current: contrasting years, 1975 through 1978. ICES Symp. on the Early Life History of Fish, Woods Hole, Mass., April 1979. Rapp. P.-v. Réun Cons. int. Explor. Mer, 178.

Lasker, R., H.M. Feder, G.H. Theilacker, and R.C. May. 1970. Feeding, growth and survival of *Engraulis mordax* larvae reared in the laboratory. Mar. Biol. 5:345–353.

Lasker, R., and J.R. Zweifel. 1978. Growth and survival of first-feeding northern anchovy (*Engraulis mordax*) in patches containing different proportions of large and small prey, p. 329–354. *In* Spatial Pattern in Plankton Communities, (ed. J. H. Steele), Plenum, New York, 470 pp.

Lillelund, K., and R. Lasker. 1971. Laboratory studies on predation by marine copepods on fish larvae. U.S. Fish. Bull. 69:655–667.

Murphy, G.T. (chairman). 1974. Report of the fourth session of the panel of experts on stock assessment on Peruvian anchoveta. Instituto del Mar del Peru (Callao), Boletin 2:605–719.

Nelson, W.R., M.C. Ingham, and W.E. Schaaf. 1977. Larval transport and year-class strength of Atlantic menhaden, *Brevoortia tyrranus*. U.S. Fish. Bull. 75:23–41.

Niiler, P.P., and E.B. Krause. 1977. One-dimensional models of the upper ocean. *In* Modeling and Prediction of the Upper Layers of the Ocean (ed. E.B. Krause), Pergamon, New York, 323 pp.

Owen, R.W. In press. Microscale plankton patchiness in the larval anchovy environment. ICES Symp. on the Early Life History of Fish, Woods Hole, Mass., April 1979. Rapp. P.-v. Réun. Cons. int. Explor. Mer 178.

Parrish, R. 1976. Environmental-dependent recruitment models and exploitation simulations of the California Current stock of Pacific mackerel (*Scomber japonicus*). Ph.D. thesis, Oregon State Univ., Corvallis, Oregon, 101 pp.

Parrish, R.H., and A.D. MacCall. 1978. Climatic variation and exploitation in the Pacific mackerel fishery. Calif. Dept. Fish and Game, Fish. Bull. 167, 110 pp.

Scura, E.D., and C.W. Jerde. 1977. Various species of phytoplankton as food for larval northern anchovy, *Engraulis mordax*, and relative nutritional value of the dinoflagellate *Gymnodinium splendens* and *Gonyaulax polyedra*. U.S. Fish. Bull. 75:577–583.

Theilacker, G.H., and R. Lasker. 1974. Laboratory studies of predation by euphausiid shrimps on fish larvae, *In* The Early Life History of Fish. (ed. J.H.S. Blaxter), pp. 287–299. Springer-Verlag, Berlin.

Valdivia, G., J.E. 1978. The anchoveta and El Niño. Rapp. P.-v. Réun. Cons. int. Explor. Mer 173:196–202.

Vlymen, W.J. 1977. A mathematical model of the relationship between larval anchovy (*Engraulis mordax*) growth, prey microdistribution and larval behavior. Env. Biol. Fish. 2:211–233.

Walsh, J.J., T.E. Whitledge, W.E. Esaias, R.L. Smith, S.A. Huntsman, H. Santander, and B.R. deMendiola. 1980. The spawning habitat of the Peruvian anchovy, *Engraulis ringens*. Deep-Sea Res. 27:1–28.

Ware, D.M., B.R. deMendiola and D.S. Newhouse. In press. Behavior of first-feeding Peruvian anchoveta larvae, *Engraulis ringens* J. ICES Symp. on the Early Life History of Fish, Woods Hole, Mass., April 1979. Rapp. P.-v. Réun. Cons. int. Explor. Mer 178.

Morphological and Functional Aspects of Marine Fish Larvae

H. G. Moser

Morphological and Functional Aspects of Marine Fish Larvae

The notion that mortality during the larval stage is a major determinant of year class strength has been a part of fisheries theory since before the turn of the century (see Marr, 1956; May, 1974; Hunter, 1976, Lasker, this volume). I have been asked to talk about the systematic aspects of the larval stage, a subject as vast and diverse as systematic ichthyology itself. The importance of diversity to fisheries science is coming into prominence as we move beyond single species concepts. Since demersal and pelagic species from all depths supply larvae to the surface waters, nowhere else in the life histories of these species is there so great a potential for interaction. One might even characterize the larval stage as that period in ontogeny when major portions of a fish fauna come together and share prey, predators, and abiotic variables. Knowledge of direct and indirect species interactions during the larval stage will play an important role in the evolution of multispecies fisheries models.

The previous lecturers have discussed larval fishes from the points of view of behavior, physiology, and ecology. I would like to focus on the morphological aspects of larval adaptation. Marine teleost larvae have evolved an enormous array of morphological specializations, such that it seems we are looking at a distinct evolutionary domain quite separate from that of the adults. It is reasonable to assume that these remarkable structural specializations are adaptive and reflect each species' solution to the challenge of survival in a complex and demanding environment. In the course of an hour I could only hope to discuss a few of the adaptations found within selected teleost groups.

A good place to start is with a problem which puzzled Aristotle and remains somewhat of a puzzle today—the life history of the European eel, *Anguilla anguilla*. Since mature gonads were never found in the freshwater adults, their reproduction remained a mystery for millenia (Schmidt, 1932). Then just before the turn of this century, two Italian scientists, Grassi and Calandruccio (1897), captured some of the leaf-like marine larvae, known as leptocephali, and kept them in an aquarium, where they turned into the transparent glass eel stage of *Anguilla* (Fig. 1). Thus, it was shown that the species was catadromous. Seven years later Johannes Schmidt captured one of these leptocephali off the Faroe Islands north of Denmark. This initiated a wide-ranging plankton sampling program that employed four Danish research vessels and numerous merchant ships in the search for the newly

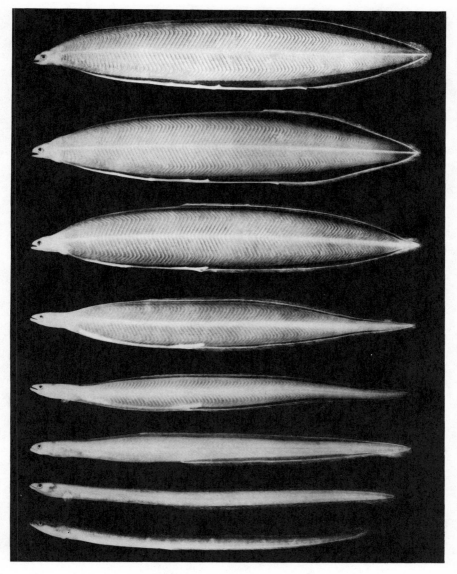

Figure 1. Transformation of the European eel, *Anguilla anguilla*, from the leptoce-phalus (at top, ca. 75 mm) to the juvenile (at bottom, ca. 64 mm). From Schmidt (1909).

91

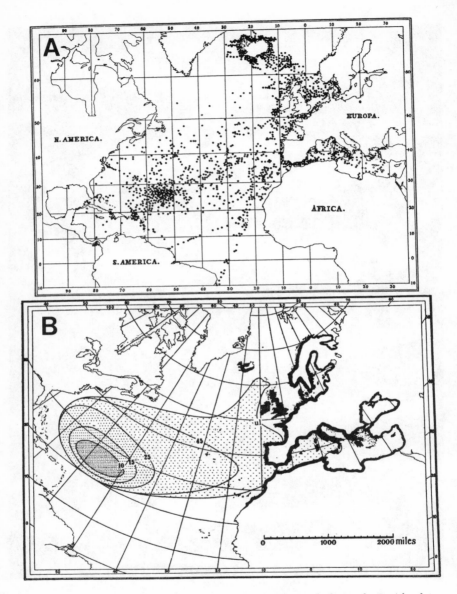

Figure 2. (A) Stations at which plankton collections were made during the Danish eel investigations, 1903-1922. (B) Areal distribution of *Anguilla anguilla* larvae based on plankton surveys. Contours indicate outer limits of occurrence of various sizes (mm) of larvae. Outermost contour refers to unmetamorphosed larvae. Black coastal strip shows distribution of juveniles and adults. From Schmidt (1925).

hatched larvae (Fig. 2). In 1922, with the discovery of newly hatched larvae in the Sargasso Sea, Schmidt concluded that ". . . the eels from Europe travel over the Atlantic to the Sargasso Sea where they spawn in the spring, and furthermore that the larvae, assisted by the North Atlantic current, make a journey in the opposite direction to Europe; a journey that lasts between two and three years" (Schmidt, 1932). Schmidt's research program was the progenitor of the type of wide-ranging ichthyoplankton survey that continues to be a valuable tool in answering fundamental questions about the life histories of marine teleosts.

Since anguillid eels are a tropical group, the migration of *A. anguilla* adults from the fresh waters of Europe to the Sargasso Sea and the slow return journey of their larvae (via the clockwise North Atlantic gyre) may have been the mechanism by which this species penetrated northward to the fresh waters of Europe. The possibility that the intercontinental journeys of this species have evolved gradually in relation to continental drift and the widening of the Atlantic during the Cretaceous, as suggested by Hulet (1978), in no way diminishes the immensity of the adaptations involved.

The nutrition of the eel larva during its journey is enigmatic since no food has ever been found in the gut of any eel leptocephalus. Furthermore, the gut is poorly differentiated and the lumen of the midgut is often occluded. The suggestion that dissolved organic compounds are absorbed directly through the epidermis is plausible since the epidermis is only from one to several cells thick and the surface cells are covered with microvilli (Hulet, 1978). Such a mode of nutrition would be remarkable since the leptocephali of some eels are the largest of all fish larvae. The leptocephalus of *Thalassenchelys coheni* attains a length of 30 cm (Smith, 1979) and a 25-cm specimen of this species in our care has a wet weight of 21 gm. The highly attenuate leptocephalus of a notacanthiform eel known as *Leptocephalus giganteus* attains a length of 184 cm (Nielsen and Larsen, 1970).

Hulet (1978) has suggested that an alternative nutritional source might be afforded by the extraordinarily large fang-like teeth typical of eel leptocephali. They could be used to puncture organisms and the protoplasmic juices could be swallowed and absorbed by the epitheleum of the esophagus and stomach. Such predaceous strategy might account for the emphasis on eye development and for the many eye specializations found among the eel leptocephali (Smith, 1979). If dissolved organic compounds are the source of leptocephalus nutrition, then the function of the huge teeth becomes problematical. Often it has been suggested that they could function in calcium metabolism. Considering the duration of the larval stage for many eels, another possibility is that they could serve as a defense against predators.

In addition to the 22 families of anguilliform eels and the three families of notacanthiform eels, leptocephali are found in the Order Elopiformes, a group which includes the tarpons, bonefishes, and ladyfishes. This was a major character used by Greenwood et al. (1966) to group the three orders into the Supraorder Elopomorpha.

Elopiform leptocephali share many morphological features with eel larvae, including the leaf-like body form, fang-like teeth, well-developed eyes, and distinct renal blood vessels, but differ markedly in having a well-developed caudal fin that is separate from the dorsal and anal fins. The caudal fin ray formula of elopiforms (10 + 9 principal rays, 4 + 3 hypurals, multiple ural centra) is also typically found in the next orders we will consider—the Clupeiformes, Salmoniformes and Myctophiformes (Ahlstrom and Moser, 1976).

Clupeiform larvae have elongate bodies with long straight intestines and are characterized by their relative uniformity and subtlety of morphological specialization (Fig. 3). Likewise, their conservative pigment patterns are dominated by serially arranged melanophores along the gut and on the ventral midline between the anus and caudal fin. It seems probable that, when expanded, the gut melanophores help conceal the larvae by masking light refracted from gut contents. Similarly, the melanistic shield which forms over the gas bladder reduces light refraction as a visual cue to potential predators. The melanistic pigment found on the oil globules of so many teleost eggs and yolk sac larvae may function in a similar way. Linear gut pigmentation and dorsal gas bladder pigment are recurrent larval characters represented in almost every teleost group in a myriad of arrangements, their universality attesting to their adaptive contribution.

Suggesting a function for the linear series of post-anal melanophores poses more of a problem. Since larvae are transparent and have a body outline that is imperceptible, or nearly so, it is unlikely that the post-anal linear series functions in concealment in the sense that Cott (1940) has shown for organisms with distinct body outlines. Moreover, if post-anal series were to function in this manner one would expect the pigment to be in the form of bars or saddles running at right angles to the body edge. Indeed, in a host of teleost species, melanistic bars and saddles are found in late larvae and pelagic juveniles, ontogenetic states where body outline is more likely to be an important cue to predators. Rather, it would seem that the distinctive post-anal melanophore series, present in so many species throughout almost every teleost group, would call the attention of potential predators. This does not negate the possibility of a protective role for post-anal pigment, since the zoological realm provides numerous examples where visual prominence of a prey species affords protection from predators.

One such example, the phenomenon of "flicker fusion," might be responsible for the widespread occurrence of post-anal melanophore series in teleost larvae as suggested by Joseph Copp (pers. comm.) of Scripps Institution of Oceanography. Describing the phenomenon in banded snakes, Shaw and Campbell (1974) state the following:

> As the snake moves forward, seeking a hiding place, the bands on its back follow one another like the spokes on a wheel. Depending on the nearness of the predator, the width of the bands and the intensity of the light on the snake . . . the results may be startling. At the very least an astigmatic

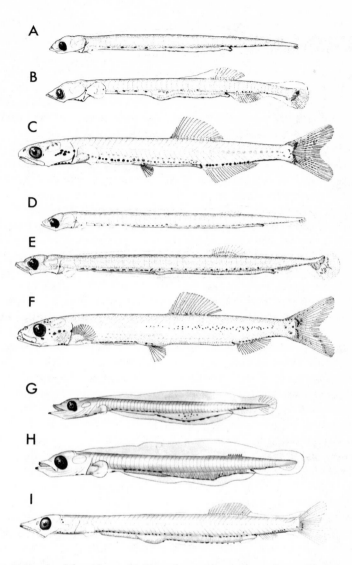

Figure 3. Larvae of clupeiforms. (A-C) northern anchovy, *Engraulis mordax*, 7.5, 11.5, 31.0 mm, from Kramer and Ahlstrom (1968); (D-F) Pacific sardine, *Sardinops sagax*, 9.1, 14.0, 31.3 mm, from Kramer (1970); (G-I) round herring, *Etrumeus teres*, 5.6, 8.2, 16.7 mm.

condition may be produced in the onlooker. Most often, however, the flicker fusion phenomenon brings a fusing in the beholder's perception of the snake's bands, a greying of them, to the point where bands and the snake no longer exist. The beholder stares fixedly at the spot where he first saw the snake and misses the fact that the snake is passing from his view.

The serially arranged post-anal melanophores of teleost larvae may function in just this manner, and indeed the obfuscation may even be more effective owing to the rapid lateral beats of the larval tail. Flicker fusion may be another reason for the widespread occurrence of serially arranged lateral gut melanophores, and the effect may be even further heightened in species where the lateral gut series and the post-anal series form a continuum. Another possible adaptive advantage of melanophores is related to the specificity of their pattern. Melanophore pattern is one of the most useful characters for distinguishing among species of teleost larvae. It is possible that unique melanophore patterns could serve an infraspecific recognition function and aid in the location and exploitation of food patches. That is, the feeding movements of one or more larvae of a species, made visible and instinctively recognizable by their unique melanistic pattern, could serve to attract other members of the species to the patch and thus provide a selective advantage. This hypothesis is consistent with the survival premium placed on patch feeding as a compensation for overall low prey densities (outlined in Dr. Hunter's lectures), and one could see how such a mechanism could lead to the proliferation of the intricate melanophore patterns, so characteristic of teleost larvae. Additionally, in many schooling fishes (e.g., clupeiforms) the onset of schooling is within the larval phase, and here again melanophore pattern may be an important factor in intraspecific recognition. One could even speculate that the behavioral mechanisms of early larval patch feeding could have been intimately involved in the evolutionary origin of schooling and other aggregation phenomena.

A remarkable feature of clupeiform larvae, which they share with elopiforms, is the phenomenon of fin migration. Fage (1920) and Lebour (1921) described how, in the late larvae of many clupeiforms, the dorsal and anal fins migrate anteriad with respect to the myomeres. Anterior migration of the dorsal fin is greatest in the European pilchard, where the fin moves forward 11 myomeres during transformation. In the herring and sprat the fin migrates 7 and 5 myomeres respectively. Anterior migration of the anal fin is less pronounced in the above species (1, 6, and 4 respectively). In the Pacific sardine the dorsal fin migrates 10 myomeres and the anal fin 6, whereas in the northern anchovy the migration is barely perceptible (dorsal, 3; anal, 1). The functional significance of fin migration is unknown; perhaps the more posterior placement of the dorsal and anal fins during the larval stage could involve them in tail beat thrust.

In salmoniform fishes the larvae have undergone an extraordinary radiation, particularly among two deep-sea groups—the argentinoid smelts and the stomiatoids. These fishes have invaded deep oceanic waters, and the morphological specializations of the larvae must have played an important role

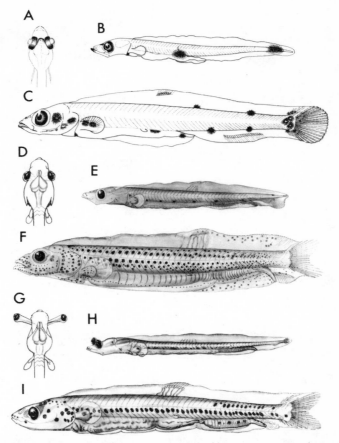

Figure 4. Larvae of argentinoid smelts showing various eye types. A-C, *Bathylagus milleri* with round eyes: (A) dorsal view of head of 10.6-mm larva, (B) 10.6-mm larva, (C) 27.5-mm larva; (D-F), *Bathylagus wesethi* with elliptical eyes, (D) dorsal view of head of 8.5-mm larva, (E) 8.8-mm larva, (F) 24.5-mm larva, from Ahlstrom (1965); G-I, *Bathylagus ochotensis* with stalked elliptical eyes, (G) dorsal view of head of 8.5-mm larva, (H) 10.2-mm larva, (I) 21.5-mm larva.

in the penetration and exploitation of this demanding environment. The fin fold has become a prominent feature and, in many salmoniforms, the dorsal and anal fins develop within the fin fold tissue at some distance from the body. The extreme is found in some argentinoids where the dorsal and anal fins form at the fin fold margin and are connected to the body by a series of hyaline strands (Fig. 4). At metamorphosis the fins become connected with the body in the normal position. The voluminous fin folds may enhance buoyancy and are probably involved in locomotion by high frequency/low amplitude vibration as Hunter (1972) has described for anchovy larvae in the S-strike position. The peripheral location of the developing dorsal and anal fins in argentinoids may serve to support the fin fold while allowing maximum freedom for vibratory locomotion.

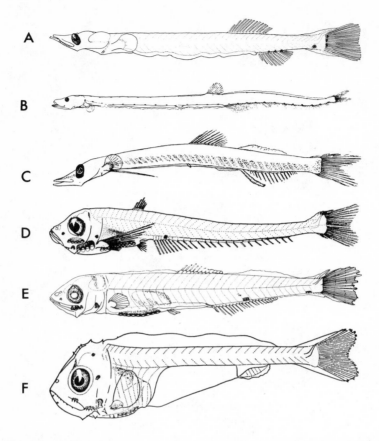

Figure 5. Larvae of stomiatoids. (A) *Vinciguerria lucetia*, 9.0 mm, from Ahlstrom and Counts (1958); (B) *Diplophos taenia*, 44 mm, from Jespersen and Taning (1919); (C) *Ichthyococcus ovatus*, 15 mm, from Jespersen and Taning (1926); (D) *Danaphos oculatus*, 22.4 mm, from Ahlstrom (1974); (E) *Maurolicus muelleri*, 10.3 mm, from Okiyama (1971); (F) *Sternoptyx* sp., 8.8 mm.

A characteristic of argentinoid larvae is the specialization of the eye. In many species the eyes have become narrowed and elliptical and in some species they are borne on stalks (Fig. 4), the possible function of which we can consider when we take up the stomiatoids.

The Stomiatoidei is dominated by two major groups, the gonostomatids and relatives and the melanostomiatids and their relatives. Gonostomatid larvae have achieved a diversity of form (Fig. 5). Some, such as the clupeoid-like *Vinciguerria*, are slender with a long intestine. *Diplophos* and *Ichthyococcus* are even more attenuate, and in the latter the posterior section of the elongate intestine trails free from the body (a feature that is widespread throughout the melanostomiatids) and the lower pectoral fin rays are extraordinarily elongate (a condition encountered in the larvae of some myctophid

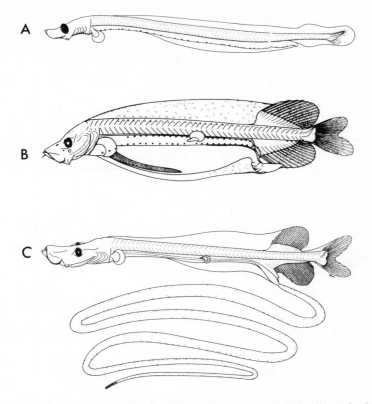

Figure 6. Larvae of stomiatoids. (A) *Stomias atriventer*, 10.0 mm; (B) *Bathophilus nigerrimus*, 21.7 mm, from Sanzo (1931); (C) Melanostomiatid, 34.5 mm.

species). In another direction, genera such as *Maurolicus* and *Danaphos* are less attenuate, have shorter intestines, and begin to develop their clumps of photophores well before transformation. The foreshortening of the gut, deepening of the body, and development of larval photophore clumps is most pronounced in the larvae of hatchet fishes, a group closely allied with the gonostomatids.

Morphological specialization reaches a zenith in larvae of the Melanostomiatidae and relatives (Fig. 6). They range from highly attenuate forms with long intestines such such as *Stomias* to rather deep-bodied forms such as *Bathopyhilus* with its voluminous sac-like intestine. The large jaws and expansive gut of the latter would appear to allow it to utilize large prey. Elongation of the gut beyond the confines of the body is a common feature of many melanostomiatid genera, and nowhere is this more apparent than in a larva tentatively identified to the genus *Leptostomias* (Fig. 6), where the gut is five times the length of the body and exceeds it in mass. One may speculate that, in this remarkable expression of alimentary dominance, digestion and absorption efficiency is improved while permitting a greater variety of prey types.

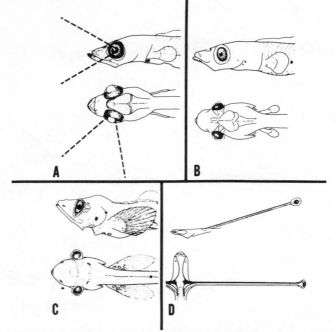

Figure 7. Various eye shapes of marine teleost larvae. (A) Round eye of *Bathylagus milleri*, lateral view (above) of 10.6-mm larva and dorsal view (below) of 9.5-mm larva; (B) Narrow sessile eye of *Bathylagus wesethi*, lateral view of 8.8-mm larva and dorsal view of 8.5-mm larva; (C) Narrow slightly stalked eye of 7.0-mm *Myctophum nitidulum* larva; (D) Markedly stalked eyes of 16-mm *Idiacanthus fasciola* larva. Figure from Weihs and Moser (1981).

Among the most specialized of all fish larvae are those of the stomiatoid family Idiacanthidae (Figs. 7 and 8). The eyes are borne on stalks that grow to one-fourth the length of the body and are then resorbed at transformation. Weihs and Moser (1981) have proposed a theory that might explain the adaptive advantage of this extraordinary specialization. If one assumes that the major causes of larval fish mortality are starvation, predation, and the interactions between them (Hunter, 1976), and that feeding and predator avoidance are largely dependent on vision, then eye specializations that improve feeding efficiency and predator avoidance are to be expected. Hunter (1972) showed that anchovy larvae notice and strike at food particles located within a 60° cone with a maximum height of about one body length and demonstrated that sighting distance and visual field are major limitations for feeding larvae.

Weihs and Moser (1981) suggest that enlargement of the visual field has evolved progressively through several stages, the first being a narrowing of a sessile round eye (Fig. 7B). In contrast to the round cup-shaped eye which lies flat in the developing orbit, the elliptical eye would have an increased rotational ability around the long axis, thus enlarging the volume observable from a given point. The next stage would be the extension of the eyes on short

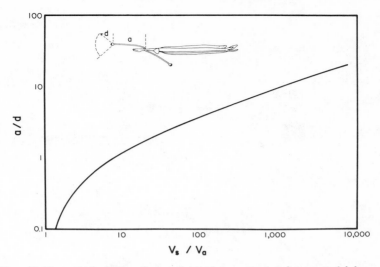

Figure 8. Theoretical relation of eye stalk length to perception distance in fish larvae. Ratio of the volume sighted by stalked eyes Vs to that covered by fully rotatable eyes attached to the head Va, versus the ratio of stalk length "a" to perception distance "d." *Idiacanthus* larva is shown to illustrate the geometrical parameters. From Weihs and Moser (1981).

stalks so that they lie just outside the margin of the eye (Fig. 7C). Such eyes could be even more freely rotated so that the observable volume would approach that of a sphere. Extension of the eyes on pedunculate stalks would further increase this volume (Fig. 7D).

These specializations raise the possibility of detecting prey from greater distances with a minimum of body motion, thus both conserving energy and reducing predator cues. Weihs and Moser (1981) calculate a tenfold increase in visual volume for elliptical eyes compared with round eyes and as much as an additional tenfold advantage for eyes borne on stalks (Fig. 8). The fact that protruding eyes have evolved independently in larvae of three families of anguilliform eels, in argentinoid and stomiatoid salmoniforms, and in the myctophiform lanternfishes points to the evolutionary value and persistence of the adaptation.

The order Myctophiformes is in some ways the most varied and interesting teleost order from the standpoint of larval development. Shallow-water benthic forms such as the synodontid lizardfishes have elongate larvae with long strait intestines, reminiscent of clupioid larvae (Fig. 9A). The large conspicuous melanistic blotches spaced evenly along the sides of the gut are characteristic of lizardfish larvae. Other benthic forms such as *Aulopus* and *Chloropthalmus* have shorter intestines with a single dorsally located melanistic blotch (Figs. 9B,C). Some deep-living benthic and benthopelagic forms have larvae with magnificent enlarged diaphanous fins (Fig. 9D). Larvae of the pelagic myctophiforms display great diversity of form. Notosudids have

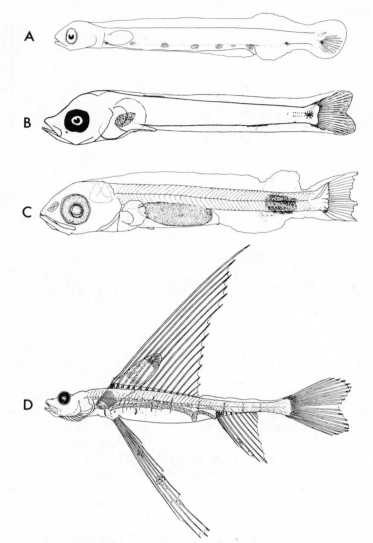

Figure 9. Larvae of demersal myctophiforms. (A) *Synodus lucioceps*, 10.5 mm; (B) *Chloropthalmus agassizi*, 9.5 mm, from Taning (1918); (C) Aulopid, 12.3 mm, from Okiyama (1974, courtesy of Springer-Verlag New York, Inc.); (D) Bathysaurid, 33 mm, from Marshall (1961).

elongate larvae with narrow elliptical eyes and curiously complex melano-phore patterns in the caudal region (Fig. 10A). Larvae of the paralepidids, midwater predators, are elongate and have extremely short intestines that lengthen markedly during the larval stage. Their characteristic pigmentation consists of large melanistic blotches that are added serially along the dorsal aspect of the gut as it elongates and may function in maintaining a masking capability commensurate with gut length (Fig. 10C-E). Larvae of another

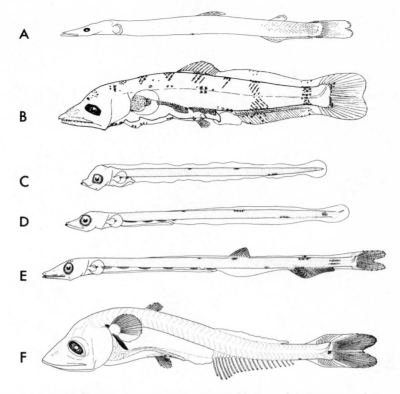

Figure 10. Larvae of midwater myctophiforms. (A) *Ahliesaurus berryi*, 30.5 mm, from Bertelsen et al. (1976); (B) *Evermannella balbo*, 11.5 mm, from Schmidt (1918); (C-E) *Lestidiops ringens*, 9.4, 16.5, 28.5 mm; (F) *Scopelarchoides nicholsi*, 23.0 mm.

midwater predatory group, the Scopelarchidae, have large jaws and a short bulbous gut that is covered by one or two very large melanistic blotches positioned directly over the saccular portion of the gut (Fig. 10F). Larvae of this group have also developed remarkably narrow eyes with pendant chorioid tissue.

In no other teleost group have the larvae explored so many pathways of evolutionary diversity as in the myctophid lanternfishes. As the largest family in the order (more than 30 genera and about 200 species), myctophids are ubiquitous in the world ocean. In a typical oceanic plankton tow about half the total fish larvae are those of lanternfishes, and Barham (1970) may be justified in suggesting that lanternfish have the largest biomass of any vertebrate group. Dr. E.H. Ahlstrom and I have been studying lanternfish larvae from a taxonomic viewpoint for over fifteen years, and our findings are detailed in four papers (Moser and Ahlstrom, 1970, 1972, 1974; Ahlstrom et al., 1976). Today I will only have time to describe some of the most prominent morphological specializations and discuss possible adaptive significance.

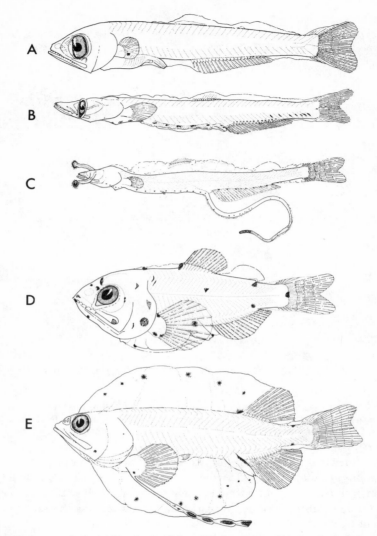

Figure 11. Larvae of myctophine lanternfishes. (A) *Protomyctophum crockeri*, 14.2 mm, from Moser and Ahlstrom (1970); (B) *Hygophum reinhardti*, 12.8 mm, ibid; (C) *Myctophum aurolaternatum*, 26.0 mm, from Moser and Ahlstrom (1974); (D) *Myctophum asperum*, 6.8 mm, ibid; (E) *Loweina rara*, 17.6 mm, from Moser and Ahlstrom (1970).

Paxton (1972) divided the family into two subfamilies, Myctophinae and Lampanyctinae, on the basis of adult osteology and photophore characters. Moser and Ahlstrom (1970) showed that characters of the larvae also divide the family, with a distribution of genera that mirrors that of Paxton. Myctophine larvae have narrow elliptical eyes and most lampanyctine larvae have round eyes, although some genera (*Triphoturus*, *Notolychnus*, *Lobianchia*) of the latter have experimented with narrowing of the eye (Figs. 11–14). Stalked eyes are found in three of the narrow-eyed myctophid genera. Practically every larval teleost body form is represented among myctophid genera, and we have been able to delineate a unique larval morph for each genus. Body form ranges from slender to stubby to leaf-like. The uncoiled intestine has distinctive transverse rugae and ranges from short, to elongate, to trailing free from the body (Fig. 11). The intestinal rugae, which are pronounced enough in myctophids and relatives to serve as an identifying character of the group, provide a mechanism for increasing the digestive and absorptive surface of an uncoiled gut.

Myctophid larvae exhibit a diversity and specificity of melanophore pattern that is unmatched among teleosts, and indeed each genus has a pigment morph that is as taxonomically useful as the structural morph. I believe that the specificity and often limited variation of pigment patterns in this group, perhaps in concert with the unique structural morphs, relate to the species recognition/patchfeeding idea presented earlier in the lecture.

A remarkable feature of lanternfish larvae is the development of one or more pairs of photophores, a character we saw in gonostomatids and sternoptychids. Larvae of almost every lanternfish species develop a photophore (later to become the middle branchiostegal photophore of juveniles and adults) below each eye. Considering the position and universality of occurrence of these photophores it is reasonable to suggest that they are functional and may lure and/or illuminate potential prey.

Additional pairs of photophores develop during the larval stage in three myctophine genera (*Benthosema, Diogenichthys, and Myctophum*) and in numerous lampanyctine genera. These additional photophore pairs appear consistently in several areas—anterior to the eye, on the outer surface of the pectoral fin penduncle, and along the ventrum. The preorbital photophores, like the branchiostegal photophores, may be utilized in feeding. The light organs on the highly motile pectoral fin base may also be involved in feeding, possibly as lures. Typical locations for the ventral organs among the various genera are below the pectoral fin base, just anterior to the developing pelvic fin, and posterior to the anus; however, the sequence of appearance of the photophores is often highly specific (Figs. 12–14). In genera such as *Diogenichthys* (Fig. 12), where the sequence of appearance of multiple photophores is highly specific, the photophore patterns may function as infraspecific recognition signals in feeding as suggested for the melanophore patterns. Since each photophore has a heavily melanistic cup, they could enhance the specificity of the melanophore patterns during the day and provide a specific luminous pattern during dim light conditions.

In larvae of two genera (*Loweina* and *Tarletonbeania*) the lowermost pectoral finrays become elongate and bear serially arranged pigmented fleshy spatulations (Fig. 11E). These elongate ornamented rays, along with some neighboring rays, are resorbed at transformation. Larvae of these same genera have voluminous fin folds which are accommodated by the posteriad

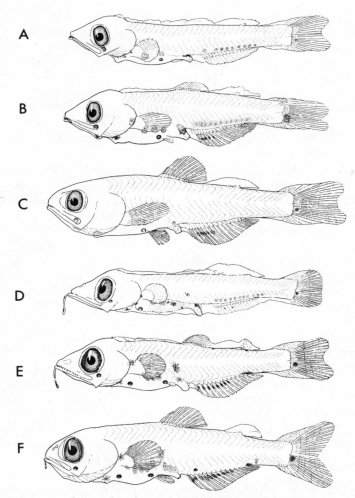

Figure 12. Larvae of myctophine lanternfishes. (A-C) *Diogenichthys lanternatus*, 6.6, 7.7, 12.3 mm; (D-F) *Diogenichthys atlanticus*, 7.2, 8.8, 12.8 mm. From Moser and Ahlstrom (1970).

displacement of dorsal and anal fins. One could postulate hydrostatic (energy saving) or nutritional (energy storage) functions for these remarkable structures. These functions could be related to orienting/stabilizing and sensory functions for the elongate rays. Another possibility is that both the voluminous fin folds and the elongate trailing pectoral fin rays enhance the apparent size of the larvae and thus function as a deterrent to potential predators. The facts that the fin folds are emphasized by an even distribution of large melanophores and that the elongate pectoral rays are provided with large melanistic spatulations support this idea.

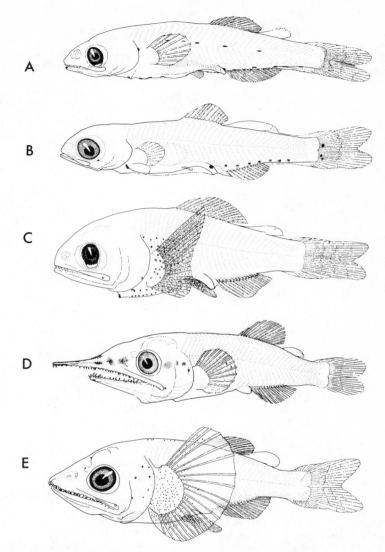

Figure 13. Larvae of lampanyctine lanternfishes. (A) *Triphoturus nigrescens*, 8.5 mm; (B) *Diaphus theta*, 6.9 mm, from Moser and Ahlstrom (1974); (C) *Lobianchia dofleini*, 8.2 mm, ibid; (D) *Lampanyctus achirus*, 13.4 mm, ibid; (E) *Lampanyctus sp.*, 9.4 mm.

Enlarged pectoral fins with supernumerary rays also occur in *Myctophum* and *Symbolophorus* and, in the other subfamily, have reached a peak of specialization in one group of *Lampanyctus* (Moser and Ahlstrom, 1974). In these species, fin enlargement is accompanied by increasing robustness of the body and prolongation of the extraordinarily toothy jaws, giving them a distinct predatory appearance (Fig. 13D, E). The body form of these larvae is

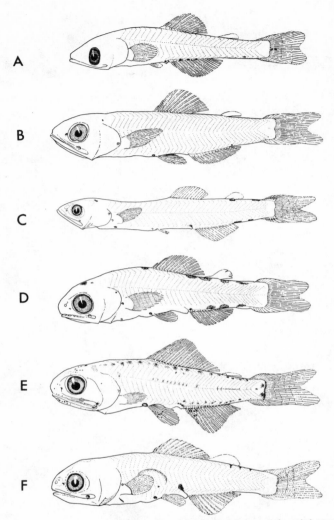

Figure 14. Larvae of notolychnine and gymnoscopeline lanternfishes. (A) *Notolychnus valdiviae*, 9.2 mm, from Moser and Ahlstrom, 1974; (B) *Ceratoscopelus townsendi*, 16.6 mm, ibid; (C) *Lepidophanes gaussi*, 13.5 mm, ibid; (D) *Lampadena urophaos*, 13.4 mm; (E) *Notoscopelus resplendens*, 16.2 mm; (F) *Lampanyctodes hectoris*, 11.7 mm, from Ahlstrom et al. (1976).

not commensurate with an S-shaped feeding strike, and one could speculate that pectoral fin thrust could play a part in the feeding strike. The "independence" of larval evolution is exemplified by these species when their robust, presumably motile and predatory larvae transform into soft-bodied, sluggish juveniles and adults. This is highlighted by the species with the largest larval pectoral fins, having the highest ray count of any myctophid, where the fin is lost completely in adults (Fig. 13E).

A major characteristic of gadiform larvae is a coiled gut, a feature found in larvae throughout the higher teleost groups. A coiled gut in the larval stage would appear to have certain advantages over the straight condition. By compressing the intestine in a mass behind the head, the digestive and propulsive systems become spatially separated and can specialize independently. Coiling would seem a natural prerequisite for the development of specialized digestive regions, separated by sphincters, that allow a more controlled rate of passage and digestion. A coiled gut with specialized functional regions is found in adults of most teleosts, whether or not their larvae have straight or coiled intestines. The development of the coiled specialized condition early in the ontogeny of most "advanced" teleosts appears to be a major evolutionary shift, permitting more efficient digestion and absorption and a greater variety of prey types.

In the gadoids, the cods and relatives, the larvae have large heads and jaws and an intestinal mass of large capacity (Fig. 15A–C). The ability of early larval stages to capture and retain prey items of a wide size range would seem advantageous to a group whose larvae are found typically in relatively deeper colder water (Sumida and Moser, 1980). In many species of morids, the pelvic fins appear early in the larval stage and develop elongate rays, sometimes ornamented with pigmented spatulations (Fig. 15E). Similarly, the macrurids develop large specialized pelvics, but also develop elongated dorsal rays and have curious paddle-shaped, highly peduncular pectoral fins (Fig. 16A).

Remarkable appendages are found in the larval stages of ophidioid fishes. Pearlfish larvae develop a highly modified dorsal appendage that bears leaf-like pigmented spatulations and in many species is directed anteriorly, possibly functioning as a lure (Fig. 16B).

What may be an example of mimicry is found in certain highly specialized ophidioid larvae that possess an ornate free trailing intestinal loop (Fig. 16C). Two such "exterilium" larvae have been reported, one taken in a trawl off Brazil (Nielsen, 1963) and the other captured alive after washing up on a beach near East London, South Africa (Fraser and Smith, 1974). A third specimen shown in Figure 16C was captured alive by a diver off New Guinea and deposited in the Scripps Institution of Oceanography Fish Collection (Cat. No. SIO 76–68). Although this larva is specifically distinct from the South African specimen (based on contrasting melanophore pattern, relative gut length, and other characters) both larvae have a fringe of fleshy cirri along the ventral edge of the intestinal loop and an arborescent appendage attached to the distal end of the loop. The cirri are marked with conspicuous large melanophores, and the resemblance of the entire structure to a siphonophore or other poisonous coelenterate prompted Fraser and Smith (1974) to suggest that the larvae may be discouraging potential predators through mimicry. One would associate such a large, highly specialized structure with prolonged pelagic life, and the authors may be correct in speculating that these are the larvae of some yet unknown group of slope or deep-sea ophidioids.

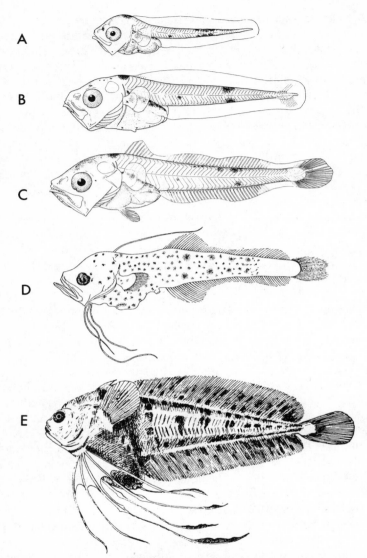

Figure 15. Young of gadiforms. (A-C) *Merluccius productus* larvae, 4.3, 7.7, 11.0 mm, from Ahlstrom and Counts (1955); (D) *Bregmaceros macclellandii* larvae, 10 mm, from D'Ancona and Cavinato (1965); (E) *Eretmophorus kleinbergi* pelagic juvenile, 105 mm, from D'Ancona (1933).

This remarkable adaptation probably arose secondarily from an adaptation associated with nourishment. Elongation of a straight intestine is common among salmoniforms and myctophiforms (Figs. 6, 11), presumably as an adaptation for improved digestion and absorption. Larvae of some higher teleosts have increased the gut mass by projecting an intestinal loop beyond the ventral body contour. This is particularly evident in bothid flatfishes such

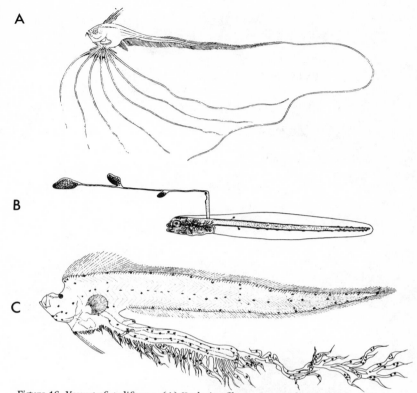

Figure 16. Young of gadiforms. (A) *Krohnius filamentosus* pelagic juvenile, 120 mm, from Sanzo (1933); (B) *Carapus acus* larva, 3.8 mm, from Padoa (1956); (C) exterilium larva, 64 mm, from Scripps Institution of Oceanography Fish Collection, Cat. No. SIO 76-68.

as *Laeops* (Amaoka, 1972) and in cynoglossid flatfishes. Presumably the trailing gut loop began as a nutritional adaptation in exterilium larvae and evolved through increasing levels of ornamentation to culminate in a structure of dual function.

Specialized elongate and often ornamented pelvic and dorsal fin rays are found widely among higher teleosts, particularly among the perciforms, pleuronectiforms, and lampridiforms. In the latter the character achieves its earliest ontogenetic expression (Figs. 17, 18). Lampridiforms produce large eggs, up to several millimeters in diameter, in which the larvae develop to an advanced state and form their elongate ornamented pelvic and anterior dorsal rays before hatching. The fact that enlarged specialized pelvic and anterior dorsal rays appear in larvae of many phylogenetically diverse higher teleosts speaks for the importance of these adaptations, whose possible functional significance was discussed earlier.

Another group with large eggs and advanced development before hatching are the atheriniform fishes—the flying fishes, sauries, and silversides. The eggs often have attachment filaments or spike-like processes, and the larvae

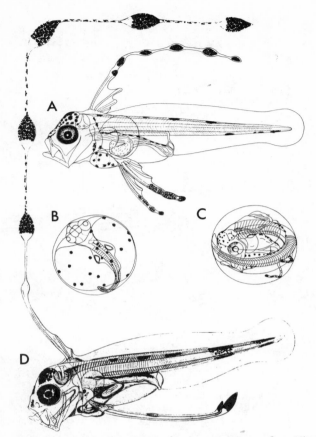

Figure 17. Larvae of lampridiforms. (A) *Trachipterus* sp., 7.6 mm, from Mito (1961); (B-C) *Trachipterus* sp., eggs, 1.8 mm, ibid; (D) *Lophotus* sp., 12.1 mm, from Sanzo (1940).

hatch with well-developed, highly functional pectoral fins and ontogenetically advanced and functional caudal fins (Fig. 19). The large egg, early fin development, and early-forming heavy melanistic pigmentation are adaptations to their stressful neustonic habitat that is characterized by high solar radiation, wind stress, and predation (by birds, invertebrates, and other fish).

The suggestion that ultraviolet radiation is the primary factor selecting for the heavy melanistic pigmentation found universally among neustonic fish larvae is supported indirectly by the experiments of John Hunter and his collaborators. Newly hatched anchovy larvae surviving four days of UV-B radiation equivalent to summertime levels off Southern California developed necrotic lesions of the eye and brain and had retarded growth and development (Hunter et al., 1979). Further experiments by Hunter et al. (in press)

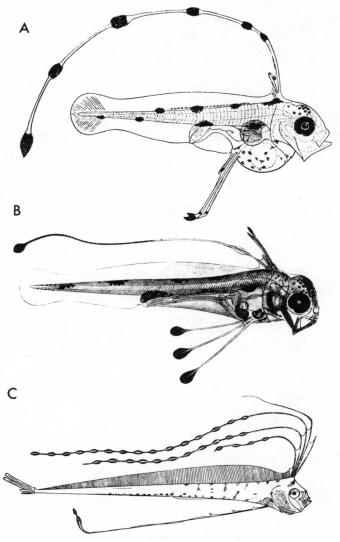

Figure 18. Larvae of lampridiforms. (A) *Zu cristatus*, 6.5 mm, from Sparta (1933a); (B-C) *Regalecus glesne*, 5.4, 45.8 mm, from Sparta (1933b).

show that developing anchovies are even more sensitive to a lower UV-B dose (equivalent to wintertime levels) given over a 12-day period, and place the LD_{50} depth at 4 m in clear oceanic water. (LD_{50} denotes the irradiation dose lethal to 50% of batch over a specified time interval.) Essentially UV-B radiation will not permit survival of the lightly pigmented anchovy larva at the surface off Southern California from March to October, while experiments on the more heavily pigmented robust larvae of Pacific mackerel show that they are twice as resistant to UV-B and could live at the surface year round.

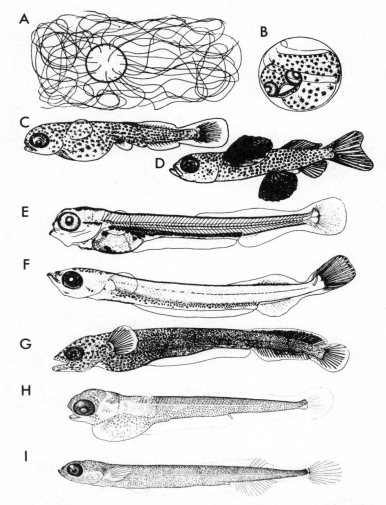

Figure 19. Larvae of atheriniforms. (A-D) *Cypselurus heterurus doderleini:* (A) egg with filaments, 1.9 mm diameter; (B) egg with 2-week-old embryo; (C) newly hatched larva, 6.3 mm; (D) 25-day-old larva, 14 mm, from Tsukahara et al. (1957); (E-F) *Hemirhamphus sajori,* 7.7 mm, 10.7 mm, from Uchida (1958); (G) *Tylosurus melanotus,* 10.2 mm, from Mito (1958); (H-I) *Cololabis saira,* 5.1, 9.9 mm.

Similar experiments have not been carried out on true neustonic species, those which live exclusively at the surface zone; however, the heavy melanism, whether it cloaks the body completely or is concentrated along the dorsum, provides protection from destructive effects of ultraviolet radiation. In addition to the heavy melanistic pigment, neustonic forms also have very heavy xanthic pigmentation that often takes the form of a solid yellow cloak and may provide additional protection from ultraviolet and visible light radiation. (For further discussion, see Perlmutter, 1961; Breder, 1962; Hempel and Weikert, 1972.)

What then is the major attraction of the neustonic zone? Zaitsev (1970) found relatively high concentrations of invertebrate plankters, of appropriate size for feeding larval fish, at the surface of the Black Sea. Similar studies yet to be carried out in oceanic waters may show that the neustonic zone is a kind of permanent food patch available to larval fish. Evolutionary requirements for successful exploitation of this "patch" appear to be a large, often attached, egg that permits advanced development before hatching, and a new-hatched larva that is relatively large, heavily pigmented, tough bodied, and capable of feeding and avoiding predators. That this neustonic morph has been achieved by species from so many phylogenetically divergent groups suggests a habitat of richness and complexity worthy of detailed study.

A major evolutionary theme in higher teleosts is spination. Within the dominant group of spiny-rayed teleosts, the Acanthopterygii, calcium metabolism and mobilization has reached a degree of perfection, and the array of fin spine, head spine, and dentitional arrangements is unmatched in complexity within the animal kingdom. The propensity to evolve specialized bony structures extends back into the larval period, where the diversity of fin and head spine specializations exceeds that of adult acanthopterygians (Figs. 20–26).

Primary sites for the accentuation and ornamentation of spines are at the anterior end of the dorsal and pelvic fins and on the head, usually posteriorly, where the head is widest and deepest, on bones such as the frontals, parietals, pterotics, posttemporals, preoperculars, and the opercular series (Figs. 20, 21). By having elongate fin and head spines at the widest region of the body the larva increases its size, from the standpoint of a potential predator, to a degree that is a function of spine length. Spines on the opercle can be extended laterally by flaring the gill covers to produce the same effect. The result is a prey item that is effectively larger, painful to ingest, thus more resistant to predation. Such a protective effect may be enormous at the size range of fish larvae, where small increments in actual or apparent prey size may have a disproportionately large effect in reducing predation by the smaller classes of organisms that prey on fish larvae.

Another effect of the elaboration of bony material into spines is to increase the specific gravity of the larva, thus posing a flotation problem. This is partially ameliorated in many larvae where structurally elegant spines are formed by supporting rods and thin serrated veins. Moreover, the center of gravity is shifted well forward in larvae with spiny heads. This appears to be compensated for in these larvae by a corresponding, more anteriad location of the gas bladder. Many acanthopterygian reef fishes (beryciform and perciform) produce larvae which inhabit open ocean waters and must have extended larval periods for their survival. They are among the spiniest of all fish larvae, leading to the often stated notion that spines enhance flotation. It is likely that increased spination in acanthopterygian fishes has the opposite effect and that flotation is the province of the gas bladder, even in fishes

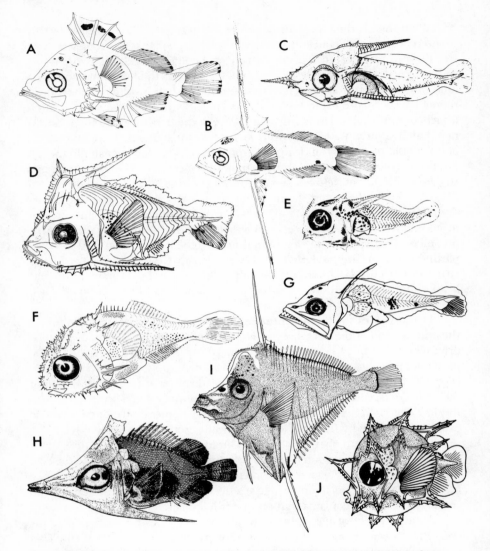

Figure 20. Larvae of acanthopterygii showing well-developed spination. (A) *Anthias gordensis*, 6.0 mm, from Kendall (1979); (B) *Epinephelus* sp., 8.4 mm, ibid; (C) *Holocentrus vexillarius*, 5.0 mm, from McKenney (1959); (D) *Antigonia rubescens*, 4.5 mm, from Uchida (1936); (E) *Dactylopterus volitans*, 3.5 mm, from Sanzo (1934); (F) *Caulolatilus princeps*, 6.0 mm; (G) *Champsodon snyderi* 4.6 mm, from Mito (1962); (H) *Forcipiger longirostris* (tholichthys stage), 17 mm, from Kendall and Goldsborough (1911); (I) acanthurid, 7 mm, from Weber (1913); (J) *Ranzania laevis*, 2.8 mm, from Tortonese (1956).

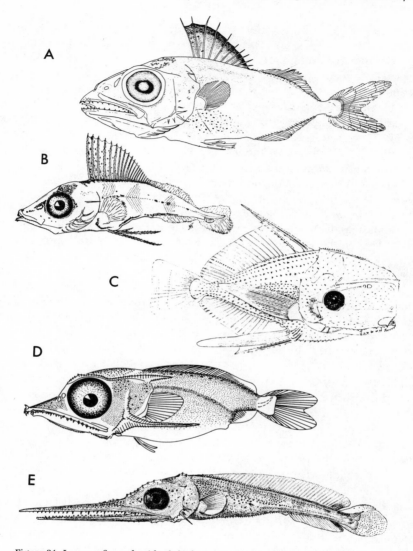

Figure 21. Larvae of scombroids. (A) *Thunnus albacares*, 14.2 mm, from Matsumoto (1958); (B) *Gempylus serpens*, 6.9 mm, from Voss (1954); (C) *Luvarus imperialis*, 11.9 mm, from De Gaetani (1930); (D) *Istiophorus americanus*, 8.1 mm, from Gehringer (1956); (E) *Xiphias gladius*, 15.6 mm, from Taning (1955).

where the bladder is lost during ontogeny. Voluminous finfolds (as in *Loweina*), distended gelatinous body envelopes (e.g., in lophiiforms and tetraodontiforms) and enlarged diaphanous fins may also serve to maintain buoyancy. It seems probable that the highly developed spination of many marine teleost larvae reflects the importance of predation as a major mortality factor during an extended larval period. In some reef and shore species a specialized pelagic juvenile stage is interposed between the larval and benthic juvenile stages. They have a unique morphology, with spines often accentuated beyond that of the larval period (Fig. 20H) and are capable of rapid transformation upon sensing bottom.

Although the adults of most spiny-rayed fishes are smooth-headed, the adults of some families within the acanthopterygian order Scorpaeniformes have complex and highly specific arrangements of head spines. Certain of these spines are well developed during the larval period and aid in identification, at least to the generic level (Moser et al., 1977; Richardson and Laroche, 1979). One group of scorpaenids, the rockfishes (*Sebastes* and relatives), have undergone extensive speciation in temperate and boreal waters. A major evolutionary trend in rockfishes is towards a more pelagic mode of life, with associated flexibility and streamlining of the body form, lightening of the skeleton, and reduction and loss of head spines. However, even the smooth-headed species have larvae with prominent head spines, many of which are lost gradually after the larval period (Moser, 1972; Moser and Ahlstrom, 1978; Richardson and Laroche, 1979; Laroche and Richardson, 1980). Retention of the ancestral pattern in their larvae suggests that the rockfishes are derived from warm-water benthic forms resembling the contemporary tropical genera, and also points out the ontogenetic and evolutionary plasticity of spine formation in this group (Moser and Ahlstrom, 1978).

Pigmentation has evolved to a high degree in larvae of acanthopterygians. In addition to the recurring types of melanistic pigment (e.g., gas bladder, oil globule, gut, post-anal series), whose possible functions were discussed earlier, unique melanopore patterns are found among the species of many groups. The possible role of pattern specificity in patch feeding was presented earlier. In addition to melanistic pigment, well-developed xanthic (yellow) pigment is encountered among the larvae of acanthopterygian fishes. The xanthophores may be in the same locations as the melanophores in a species, or they may be arranged in a distinctly different pattern, thus affording the larva two separate and unique patterns of pigmentation (see Mito, 1960, 1963, for examples). Where the xanthophores co-occur with the melanophores they may enhance the melanophore pattern signal, and where they are complementary they could serve to increase the specificity of the overall pattern. Xanthophore patterns seem to be best developed in coastal fishes, where reduced water clarity may obscure the melanistic pattern. An interesting feature of xanthophores is that they appear brown or black when viewed in transmitted light and have the appearance of melanophores when illuminated from the back. Much is to be learned about this dual capacity

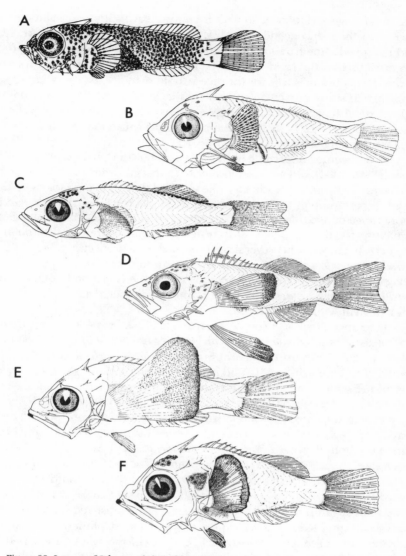

Figure 22. Larvae of *Sebastes*. (A) *S. oblongus*, 14 mm, from Fujita (1958); (B) *S. mac-donaldi*, 9.0 mm, from Moser et al. (1977); (C) *S. jordani*, 15.5 mm, ibid; (D) *S. pau-cispinis*, 14.0 mm, ibid; (E) *S. levis*, 10.4 mm, ibid; (F) *S. melanostomus*, 8.2 mm, from Moser and Ahlstrom (1978).

and about the synthesis, arrangement, and role of xanthic pigment in fish larvae.

The flatfishes (Pleuronectiformes) are a large group of fishes which have become highly specialized for life on the seafloor and have both eyes on the side away from the substrate. In all flatfishes the eyes are symmetrical during the larval stage and migrate to their asymmetrical position during metamorphosis. In the pleuronectids (the highly successful group of northern seas) and the soleids (the true soles of temperate and tropical waters), the left eye migrates over to the right side of the head and the left side faces the substrate. The opposite is true for the diverse bothid and cynoglossid flatfishes of tropical and subtropical waters. Early in the larval stage, flatfish are not unlike larvae of typical acanthopterygians; however, they soon develop a deep, laterally compressed body form and a markedly coiled gut that is positioned well forward in the body.

Pleuronectiform larvae have a large array of morphological specializations (Figs. 24–26). The most prominent specialization is size. Size has played an important evolutionary role in larval flatfishes, perhaps more than in any other group of teleosts. To begin with, pleuronectiform eggs span the entire range of teleost egg size. Species with small eggs (ca. 0.6 mm in diameter), approaching the lower limit of teleost egg size, are found throughout the flatfish groups, and several species in the pleuronectid genera *Hippoglossus*, *Hippoglossoides*, and *Reinhardtius* approach the upper size limit for pelagic teleost eggs. Most notably, the eggs of the Greenland halibut, *Reinhardtius hippoglossoides*, are 4.0–4.5 mm in diameter and the larvae are 10–16 mm at hatching (Jensen, 1935).

The range of sizes encountered among flatfish larvae is greater than in any teleost group. Larvae of the achirine soles are among the smallest of all teleost larvae. For example, larvae of the lined sole, *Achirus lineatus* (Fig. 26), are 1.6 mm long at hatching and complete metamorphosis before they are 5.0 mm (Houde et al., 1970). In contrast, the larvae of some pleuronectids and bothids attain very large sizes (Figs. 24–25). Dover sole (*Microstomus pacificus*) larvae exceed 60 mm in length, and those of the rex sole (*Glyptocephalus zachirus*) reach a maximum of about 90 mm (Pearcy et al., 1977). Larvae of bothid genera such as *Kamoharaia*, *Laeops*, and *Taeniopsetta* reach sizes in the 70–90 mm size range, and those of *Chascanopsetta* exceed 100 mm (Nielsen, 1963; Amaoka, 1970, 1971, 1972). Barham (1966) observed from a submarine a remarkable bothid larva that he estimated to be more than 220 mm in length. The point is that, in flatfish, egg and larval size (and accordingly age) has been explored as a major adaptation.

Shallow or estuarine forms, such as the achirine soles, have solved the problem of recruitment of planktonic larvae to an areally limited bottom habitat by reducing the length and therefore the dispersal of the larval state. In contrast, the deepest living species have protracted the larval state through sustained growth, thus increasing the probability of settling success following shoreward and bottomward drift or migration. Not only is the time interval available for settling extended, but the length and time range over which metamorphosis can occur is increased in the species with larger larvae. This phenomenon is clearly demonstrated among the species of *Pleuronichthys* where there is a gradation in size at metamorphosis (Fig. 24). The bay and nearshore species transform and settle at small sizes, and the deeper water

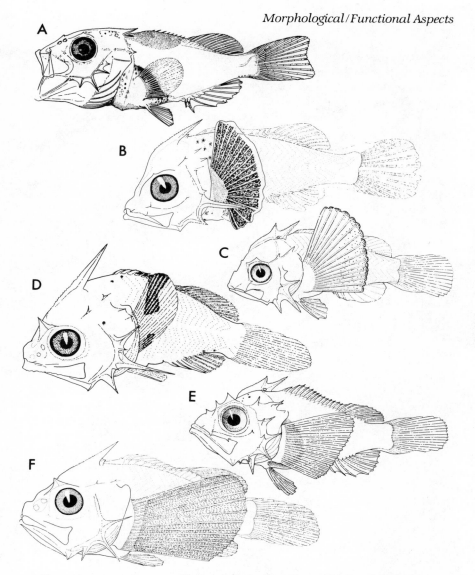

Figure 23. Larvae of scorpaenids. (A) *Helicolenus dactylopterus*, 19.0 mm, from Taning (1961); (B) *Scorpaena guttata*, 6.2 mm, from Moser et al. (1977); (C) *Scorpaenodes xyris*, 6.2 mm, ibid; (D) *Pontinus* sp., 5.0 mm, ibid; (E) *Sebastolobus altivelis*, 11.2 mm, ibid; (F) *Ectreposebastes imus*, 6.7 mm, ibid.

species attain larger sizes before metamorphosis (Sumida et al., 1979).

The heavily pigmented larvae of *Pleuronichthys* are taken frequently in our neuston collections. Particularly prominent in these collections are fully transformed juveniles of the deeper water species, *P. coenosus* and *P. decurrens*. Since transformed flatfish have a blind side, they would be at a disadvantage in finding food and avoiding predators prior to settling. These disadvantages might be reduced in the neustonic zone, where juvenile

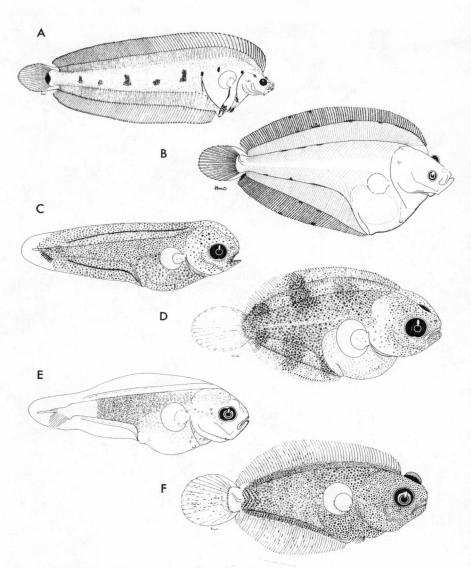

Figure 24. Larvae of pleuronectid flatfishes. (A) *Glyptocephalus zachirus*, 47.0 mm after Ahlstrom and Moser (1975); (B) *Microstomus pacificus*, 14.6 mm; (C) *Pleuronichthys decurrens*, 9.7 mm, from Sumida et al. (1979); (D) *P. decurrens*, 10.0 mm, showing initial eye migration, ibid; (E) *Pleuronichthys ritteri*, 5.6 mm, ibid; (F) *P. ritteri*, 6.4 mm, showing initial eye migration, ibid.

Pleuronichthys could feed efficiently on surface organisms while gaining some measure of disguise from their orientation just below the sea boundary. In effect, they may have "settled" temporarily at one surface before they arrive at water of appropriate depth for benthic settling.

The fact that flatfish species and genera with large larvae typically have broader zoogeographic distributions has led to the suggestion that increased

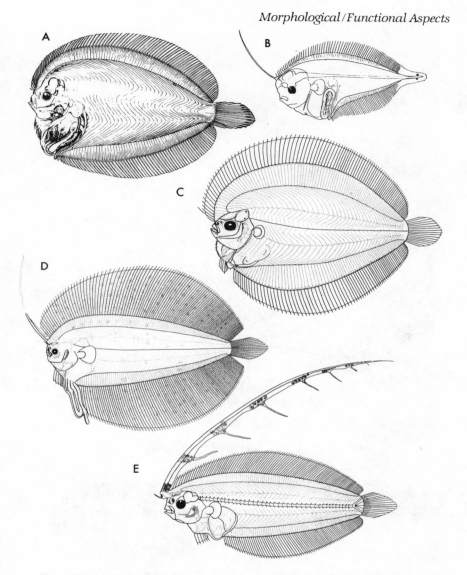

Figure 25. Larvae of bothid flatfishes. (A) *Bothus constellatus*, 27.1 mm; (B) *B. constellatus*, 6.2 mm; (C) *Taeniopsetta ocellata*, 59 mm, from Amaoka (1970); (D) *Laeops kitaharae*, 79 mm, from Amaoka (1972); (E) *Arnoglossus japonicus*, 30.5 mm, from Amaoka (1973).

size is a dispersal mechanism that increases species fitness (Brunn, 1937). An alternative hypothesis is that wide dispersal is a secondary consequence of increased larval size (and time) as a solution for the problem of larval settling in deep-living species.

The deep, sometimes leafshaped, body form of many larger flatfish larvae is related to a major locomotive adaptation. The deep body form results

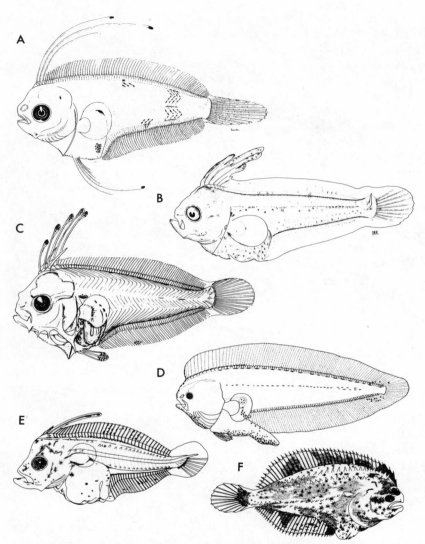

Figure 26. Larvae of paralichthyid, cynoglossid and soleid flatfishes. (A) *Citharichthys platophrys*, 8.6 mm; (B) *Paralichthys californicus*, 5.9 mm; (C) *Syacium ovale*, 6.5 mm; (D) *Symphurus atricauda*, 12.8 mm; (E) *Achirus lineatus*, 3.1 mm, from Houde et al. (1970); (F) *A. lineatus*, newly transformed specimen, 5.4 mm, ibid.

from the laterally compressed nature of the epaxial and hypaxial muscle masses, a widening of the dorsal and anal fin pterygiophore zones, and a lengthening of the dorsal and anal fin rays. The relative contribution of the pterygiophore zone to total body depth varies among species of flatfish. In some large deep-bodied larvae it contributes more to the total body depth than does the body musculature zone. Since flatfish larvae are extremely thin-bodied and flexible, the pterygiophore zone essentially enlarges the dorsal and anal fins, thus enhancing the power and precision of fin undulation. Barham's (1966) account of undulatory propulsion in the large unidentified flatfish larva and his estimate of 0.5 m/sec swimming speed highlight the importance of dorsal and anal fin undulation, with its associated enhanced directionality, in larval flatfish locomotion.

Further specialization of the dorsal fin is seen in bothid larvae (Fig. 25), which develop an elongate, sometimes ornamented, second dorsal ray and in many paralichthyid larvae (Fig. 26) which have a group of elongate anterior dorsal rays forming a comb-like structure. The elongate ray in bothids might have a sensory function. Barham (1966) observed that the dorsal fin "comb" was held erect during undulatory locomotion of his giant larva, and John Butler and I have observed that the smaller dorsal fin comb of reared California halibut (*Paralichthys californicus*) larvae is also held erect during locomotion, suggesting that the comb may function as a rudder during undulatory locomotion and possibly as a stabilizing vane during caudal-fin-generated feeding strikes. In some paralichthyid larvae, the pelvic fins are also enlarged by ray elongation and may function during undulatory locomotion.

Another possible function for the elongate dorsal ray in bothids and the elongate dorsal and pelvic rays in paralichthyids is to increase the apparent size of the larva as a means of reducing predation. In some species of the bothid genus *Arnoglossus* (Fig. 25E), the produced dorsal ray bears fleshy streamers and heavy pigmentation, and in paralichthyids such as *Citharichthys* and *Syacium* (Fig. 26A,C), the tips of the elongate dorsal and pelvic rays have pigmented spatulations. These highly emphasized rays produce the effect of a second body contour and thus may increase the apparent size of the larva, as suggested earlier in the lecture for groups with similar larval appendages.

Other specializations of flatfish larvae include a vast array of head spine patterns, the secondary elongation of the gut coil to a trailing condition in bothids and cynoglossids, and the development of highly complex and specific melanistic pigment patterns, particularly in the pleuronectids (Figs. 24–26).

One could not leave a survey of teleost larval specialization without mentioning the remarkable larvae of lophiiform angler fishes (Fig. 27). Goosefish (*Lophius*) larvae, with their elongate dorsal and pelvic fin rays, huge pectoral fins, balloon-like outer skin, and large size are among the most beautiful of all fish larvae (Fig. 27A). The adaptations are associated with prolonged pelagic life and presumably are related to the evolution of deeper-living benthic species, as suggested above for deep-water flatfish. Ontogeny in the deep-water pelagic angler fishes (Ceratioidei) is fully described in Bertelsen's (1951) definitive monograph. Dr. Richard Rosenblatt's suggestion (pers. comm.) that the deep water pelagic angler fishes are neotenic derivatives of benthic coastal forms via extended pelagic larval or juvenile stages is fascinating to consider; the gelatinous balloon-like skin of adult ceratioids

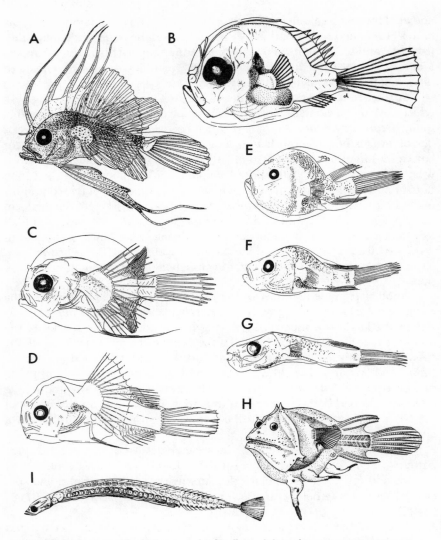

Figure 27. Larvae of lophiiforms and *Schindleria*. (A) *Lophius piscatorius*, 26 mm, from Taning (1923); (B) *Histrio histrio*, 2.0 mm, from Adams (1960); (C) *Caulophryne jordani*, 9.5 mm, from Bertelsen (1951); (D) *C. jordani*, 10.0-mm metamorphic male, ibid.; (E) *Cryptosaras couesi*, 11.8-mm female, ibid.; (F) *C. couesi*, 9.8-mm metamorphic male, ibid.; (G) *C. couesi*, 14.3 mm, oldest free-living stage of male, ibid.; (H) *Edriolychnus schmidti*, 70-mm adult female with 3 parasitic males, ibid.; (I) *Schindleria praematurus*, 15-mm ripe female, from Brunn (1940).

could be considered a retention of a pelagic larval character. The larvae of many ceratioids are sexually dimorphic and the mature males are distinctly larvoid in appearance. The reduction of ceratioid males to short-lived gamete carriers and the further reduction to attached "parasitic" sperm sacs in at least four families are well known. Larvoid males are also found in the stomiatoid, *Idiacanthus*, and the gobiid genus *Crystallogobius* appears neotenic. This tendency reaches the extreme in *Schindleria* (Fig. 27I), where adults range from 10.5 to 20.5 mm SL, weigh 2.0–8.0 mg, and in all appearances are larvae (Brunn, 1940). Here neoteny has been explored to the lower limits of vertebrate size and marks a convenient point to end the lecture.

Acknowledgments

I would like to thank Dr. Richard Harbison (Woods Hole Oceanographic Institution) for the loan of the melanostomiatid larva illustrated in Figure 6C and Dr. Richard Rosenblatt (Scripps Institution of Oceanography) for the loan of the exterilium larva shown in Figure 16C. George Mattson illustrated Figures 3G–I, 4D–I, 14D and E, 19H and I, 25A and B, 26C and D. Henry Orr illustrated Figures 4A–C, 5F, 9A, 10C–F, 20F, 24B, 26B. Barbara Sumida Mac-Call illustrated Figures 6A–C, 24A, 26A.

References

Adams, J.A. 1960. A contribution to the biology and post larval development of the sargassum fish, *Histrio histrio* (Linnaeus), with a discussion of the *Sargassum* complex. Bull. Mar. Sci. 10(1):55–82.

Ahlstrom, E.H. 1965. Kinds and abundance of fishes in the California Current based on egg and larval surveys. Calif. Coop. Oceanic Fish. Invest. Rep. 10:31–52.

———. 1974. The diverse patterns of metamorphosis in gonostomatid fishes. *In* The Early Life History of Fish (ed. J.H.S. Blaxter). Springer-Verlag, NY, 765 pp.

Ahlstrom, E.H., and R.C. Counts. 1955. Eggs and larvae of the Pacific hake *Merluccius productus*. U.S. Fish. Bull. 56:295–329.

———. 1958. Development and distribution of *Vinciguerria lucetia* and related species in the eastern Pacific. U.S. Fish. Bull. 58:363–416.

Ahlstrom, E.H., and H.G. Moser. 1975. Distributional atlas of fish larvae in the California Current region: Flatfishes, 1955 through 1960. CalCOFI Atlas No. 23, 207 pp.

———. 1976. Eggs and larvae of fishes and their role in systematic investigations and in fisheries. Rev. Trav. Inst. Pêches marit. 40(3–4):379–398.

Ahlstrom, E.H., H.G. Moser, and M.J. O'Toole. 1976. Development and distribution of larvae and early juveniles of the commercial lanternfish, *Lampanyctodes hectoris* (Gunther), off the west coast of southern Africa with a discussion of phylogenetic relationships of the genus. Bull. Southern California Acad. Sci. 75:138–152.

Amaoka, K. 1970. Studies on the larvae and juveniles of the sinistral flounders—I. *Taeniopsetta ocellata* (Gunther). Jap. J. Ichthyol. 17(3):95–104.

———. 1971. Studies on the larvae and juveniles of the sinistral flounders—II. *Chascanopsetta lugubris*. Jap. J. Ichthyol. 18(1):25–32.

———. 1972. Studies on the larvae and juveniles of the sinistral flounders—III. *Laeops kitaharae*. Jap. J. Ichthyol. 19(3):154–165.

————. 1973. Studies on the larvae and juveniles of the sinistral flounders—IV. *Arnoglossus japonicus*. Jap. J. Ichthyol. 20(3):145–156.

Barham, E.G. 1966. An unusual pelagic flatfish observed and photographed from a diving saucer. Copeia 1966(4):865–867.

————. 1970. Deep sea fishes: Lethargy and vertical orientation. *In* Proceedings of an International Symposium on Biological Sound Scattering in the Ocean (ed. G.B. Farquhar). U.S. Naval Oceanography Office, Washington, DC, 629 pp.

Bertelsen, E. 1951. The ceratioid fishes. Ontogeny, taxonomy, distribution and biology. Dana Rep. 39, 276 pp.

Bertelsen, E., G. Krefft, and N.B. Marshal. 1976. The fishes of the family Notosudidae. Dana Rep. 86, 114 pp.

Breder, C.M. 1962. On the significance of transparency in osteichthid fish eggs and larvae. Copeia 1962(3):561–567.

Brunn, A.F. 1937. *Chascanopsetta* in the Atlantic, a bathypelagic occurrence of a flatfish. Vidensk. Medd. Dan. Naturh. Foren. Kbh. 101:125–135.

————. 1940. A study of a collection of the fish *Schindleria* from South Pacific waters. Dana Rep. 21, 12 pp.

Cott, H.B. 1940. Adaptive Coloration in Animals. Methuen and Co. Ltd., London, 508 pp.

D'Ancona, U. 1933. Ordine: Anacanthini, Famiglia 1: Gadidae. *In* uova, larve e stadi giovanili di Teleostei, Fauna e Flora del Golfo di Napoli, Monogr. 38(2):178–255.

D'Ancona, U., and G. Cavinato. 1965. The fishes of the family Bregmacerotidae. Dana Rep. 64, 92 pp.

DeGaetani, D. 1930. Stadio giovanile di *Astrodermus elegans*. Bp. Mem. R. Com. Talass. Ital. 181, 8 pp.

Fage, L. 1920. Eugraulidae, Clupeidae. Rep. Danish Oceanogr. Exped. Mediterr. 2(A9), 140 pp.

Fraser, T.H., and M.M. Smith. 1974. An exterilium larval fish from South Africa with comments on its classification. Copeia 1974(4):886–892.

Fujita, S. 1958. On the egg development and larval stages of a viviparous scorpaenid fish, *Sebastes oblongus* Gunther. Bull. Jap. Soc. Sci. Fish. 24 (6 and 7):475–479.

Gehringer, J.W. 1956. Observations on the development of the Atlantic sailfish, *Istiophorus americanus* (Cuvier) with notes on an unidentified species of istiophorid. U.S. Fish. Bull. 57:139–171.

Grassi, G., and S. Calandruccio. 1897. Descrizione d'un *Leptocephalus brevirostris* in via di transformarsi in *Anguilla vulgaris*. Atti. Accad. Lincei 5 (ser. 6, pt. 1):239–240.

Greenwood, P.H., D.E. Rosen, S.H. Weitzman, and G.S. Myers. 1966. Phyletic studies of teleostean fishes, with a provisional classification of living forms. Bull. Amer. Mus. Nat. Hist. 131(4):341–355.

Hempel, G., and H. Weikert. 1972. The neuston of the subtropical and boreal Northeastern Atlantic Ocean. A review. Mar. Biol. 13(1):70–88.

Houde, E., C.R. Futch and R.D. Detwyler. 1970. Development of the lined sole, *Archirus lineatus*, described from laboratory-reared and Tampa Bay specimens. Fla. Dep. Nat. Res. Mar. Res. Lab. Tech. Ser., No. 62, 43 pp.

Hulet, W.H. 1978. Structure and functional development of the eel leptocephalus *Ariosoma balearicum* (De La Roche, 1809). Phil. Trans. Royal Soc. Lond. B. Biol. Sci. 282(987):107–138.

Hunter, J.R. 1972. Swimming and feeding behavior of larval anchovy, *Engraulis mordax*. U.S. Fish. Bull. 70:821–838.

————. 1976. Report of a colloquium on larval fish mortality studies and their relation to fishery research. U.S. Dept. Commer., NOAA Tech. Rep. NMFS Circ. 395, 5 pp.

Hunter, J.R., J.H. Taylor, and H.G. Moser. 1979. The effect of ultraviolet irradiation on eggs and larvae of the northern anchovy, *Engraulis mordax*, and the Pacific mackerel, *Scomber japonicus*, during the embryonic stage. Photochem. Photobiol. 29:325–338.

Hunter, J.R., S.E. Kaupp, and J.H. Taylor. In press. Effects of solar radiation and artificial UV-B radiation on larval northern anchovy, *Engraulis mordax*. Photochem. Photobiol.

Jensen, A.S. 1935. The Greenland halibut (*Reinhardtius hippoglossoides*), its development and migrations. K. Dan. Vidensk. Selsk. Skr. 9(4):1–32.

Jespersen, P., and A.V. Taning. 1919. Some Mediterranean and Atlantic Sternoptychidae. Preliminary note. Vidensk. Medd. Dan. Naturh. Foren., Kbh. 70:215–226.

———. 1926. Mediterranean Sternoptychidae. Rep. Danish Oceanogr. Exped. 1908–10, 2(A 12), 59 pp.

Kendall, A.W. 1979. Morphological comparisons of North American seabass larvae (Pisces: Serranidae). U.S. Dep. Commer., NOAA Tech. Rep. NMFS Circ. 428, 50 pp.

Kendall, W.C., and E.L. Goldsborough. 1911. Reports on the scientific results of the expedition to the tropical Pacific, in charge of Alexander Agassiz, by the U.S. Fish Commission Steamer "Albatross," from August 1899 to March 1900, Commander Jefferson F. Moser, USN Commanding. XIII. The Shore fishes. Mem. Mus. Comp. Zool., Harvard, 26(7):293–344.

Kramer, D. 1970. Distributional atlas of fish eggs and larvae in the California Current region: Pacific sardine, *Sardinops caerulea* (Girard), 1951 through 1966. CalCOFI Atlas No. 12, 277 pp.

Kramer, D., and E.H. Ahlstrom. 1968. Distributional atlas of fish larvae in the California Current region: Northern anchovy, *Engraulis mordax* Girard, 1951 through 1965. CalCOFI Atlas No. 9, 269 pp.

Laroche, W.A., and S.L. Richardson. 1980. Development and occurrence of larvae and juveniles of the rockfishes *Sebastes flavidus* and *Sebastes melanops* (Scorpaenidae) off Oregon. U.S. Fish. Bull. 77(4):901–924.

Lebour, M.V. 1921. The larval and post-larval stages of the pilchard, sprat and herring from the Plymouth district. J. Mar. Biol. Assoc. U.K. 12:427–457.

Marr, J.C. 1956. The "critical period" in the early life history of marine fishes. J. Cons. int. Explor. Mer 21:160–170.

Marshall, N.B. 1961. A young *Macristium* and the ctenothrissid fishes. Bull. British Mus. (Nat. Hist.), Zool., 7:353–370.

Matsumoto, W.M. 1958. Descriptions and distribution of larvae of four species of tuna in central Pacific waters. U.S. Fish. Bull. 58:31–72.

May, R.C. 1974. Larval mortality in marine fishes and the critical period concept. *In* The Early Life History of Fish (ed. J.H.S. Blaxter), Springer-Verlag, NY, 765 pp.

Mito, S. 1958. Eggs and larvae of *Tylosaurus melanotus* (Bleeker) (Belonidae). In K. Uchida et al., Studies on the Eggs, Larvae and Juveniles of the Japanese Fishes. J. Fac. Agric., Kyushu Univ., Ser I, 89 pp.

———. 1960. Keys to the pelagic fish eggs and hatched larvae found in the adjacent waters of Japan. Sci. Bull. Fac. Agric. Kyushu Univ. 18(1):71–94.

———. 1961. Pelagic fish eggs from Japanese waters—II. Lamprida, Zeida, Mugilina, Scombrina, Carangina and Stromateina. Sci. Bull. Fac. Agric. Kyushu Univ. 18(4):451–465.

———. 1962. On the egg development and early larvae of a trachinoid fish, *Champsodon snyderi* Franz. Bull. Jap. Soc. Sci. Fish 28(5):499–503.

————. 1963. Pelagic fish eggs from Japanese waters—III. Percina, VIII. Cottina, IX. Echeneida and Pleuronectida. Japanese J. Ichthyol. 11:39–102.

Moser, H.G. 1972. Development and distribution of the rockfish, *Sebastes macdonaldi* (Eigenmann and Beeson, 1893), family Scorpaenidae off southern California and Baja California. U.S. Fish. Bull. 70:941–958.

Moser, H.G., and E.H. Ahlstrom. 1970. Development of lanternfishes (Family Mycto- phidae) in the California Current. Part I. Species with narrow-eyed larvae. Bull. Los Ang. Cty. Mus. Nat. Hist. Sci. 7, 145 pp.

————. 1972. Development of the lanternfish, *Scopelopsis multipunctatus* Brauer 1906, with a discussion of its phylogenetic position in the family Myctophidae and its role in a proposed mechanism for the evolution of photophore patterns in lan- ternfishes. U.S. Fish. Bull. 70:541–564.

————. 1974. Role of larval stages in systematic investigations of marine teleosts: the Myctophidae, a case study. U.S. Fish. Bull. 72:391–413.

————. 1978. Larvae and pelagic juveniles of blackgill rockfish, *Sebastes melanos- tomus*, taken in mid-water trawls off southern California and Baja California. J. Fish. Res. Board Can. 35:981–996.

Moser, H.G., E.H. Ahlstrom, and E.M. Sandknop. 1977. Guide to the identification of scorpionfish larvae in the eastern Pacific with notes on species of *Sebastes* and *Heli- colenus* from other oceans. U.S. Dep. Commer., NOAA Tech. Rep. NMFS Circ. 402, 71 pp.

McKenney, T.W. 1959. A contribution to the life history of the squirrel fish *Holo- centrus vexillarius* Poey. Bull. Mar. Sci. 9(2):174–221.

Nielsen, J.G. 1963. Description of two large unmetamorphosed flatfish larvae (Hetero- somata). Vidensk. Medd. Dan. Naturh. Foren. Kbh. 125:401–406.

Neilsen, J.G., and V. Larsen. 1970. Remarks on the identity of the giant Dana eel-larva. Vidensk. Medd. Dan. Naturh. Foren. Kbh. 133:149–157.

Okiyama, M. 1971. The early life history of the gonosomatid fish, *Maurolicus muelleri* (Gmelin), in the Japan Sea. Bull. Jap. Sea Rep. Fish. Res. Lab. 23:21–52.

————. 1974. The larval taxonomy of the primitive myctophiform fishes. *In* The Early Life History of Fish (ed. J.H.S. Blaxter). Springer-Verlag, NY, 765 pp.

Padoa, E. 1956. Famiglia 9. Carapidae. In Uova, larve e stadi giovanili de Teleostei, Fauna e Flora del Golfo del Napoli, Monogr. 38(3):761–774.

Paxton, J.R. 1972. Osteology and relationships of the lanternfishes (Family Myctophi- dae). Bull. Los Angeles County Mus. Nat. Hist. Sci. 13, 81 pp.

Pearcy, W.G., M.J. Hosie, and Sally L. Richardson. 1977. Distribution and duration of pelagic life of Dover sole, *Microstomus pacificus*; rex sole, *Glyptocephalus zachirus*; and petrale sole, *Eopsetta jordani*; in waters off Oregon. U.S. Fish. Bull. (1):173–183.

Perlmutter, A. 1961. Possible effect of lethal visible light on year class fluctuations of aquatic animals. Science 133:1081-1082.

Richardson, S.L., and W.A. Laroche. 1979. Development and occurrence of larvae and juveniles of the rockfishes *Sebastes crameri*, *Sebastes pinniger*, and *Sebastes helvo- maculatus* (family Scorpaenidae) off Oregon. U.S. Fish. Bull. 77:1-46.

Sanzo, L. 1931. Sottordine: Stomiatoidei. *In* Uova, larve e stadi giovanili di Teleostei, Fauna e Flora de Golfo di Napoli, Monogr. 38(1):42-92.

————. 1933. Ordine: Anacanthini Famiglia 2: Macruridae. *In* Uova, larve e stadi gio- vanili di Teleostei, Fauna e Flora del Golfo di Napoli, Monogr. 38(2):255-265.

————. 1934. Uova stadi larvali e giovanili di *Dactylopterus volitans* L. Mem. R. Com. Talass. Ital. 207, 26 pp.

————. 1940. Uova e larva appena schiusa di *Lophotes cepedianus* (Giorna). Mem. R. Com. Talass. Ital. 267, 6 pp.

Schmidt, J. 1909. Remarks on the metamorphosis and distribution of the larvae of the eel (*Anguilla vulgaris*, Turt.). Med. Komm. Havuunders., Ser. Fisk. 3(3):1–17.

―――. 1918. Argentinidae, Microstomidae, Opisthoproctidae, Mediterranean Odontostomidae. Rep. Danish Oceanogr. Exped. 1908-10, 2(A5), 40 pp.

―――. 1925. The breeding places of the eel. Ann. Rep. Smithsonian Inst. 1924:279-316.

―――. 1932. Danish Eel Investigations During 25 Years (1905-1930). Carlsberg Foundation, Copenhagen, 16 pp.

Shaw, C.E., and S. Campbell. 1974. Snakes of the American West. Alfred A. Knopf, Inc., New York, 330 pp. Reprinted with permission from the publisher.

Smith, D.G. 1979. Guide to the leptocephali (Elopiformes, Anguilliformes, and Notacanthiformes). U.S. Dep. Commer., NOAA Tech. Rep. NMFS Circ. 424, 39 pp.

Sparta, A. 1933a. Ordine: Allotriognathi. Famiglia 1: Trachipteridae. *In* Uova, larve e stadi giovanili di Teleostei, Fauna e Flora de Golfo di Napoli, Monogr. 38(1):267-275.

―――. 1933b. Ordine: Allotriognathi. Famiglia: Regalecidae. *In* Uova, larve e stadi giovanili di Teleostei, Fauna e Flora de Golfo di Napoli, Monogr. 38(1):276-279.

Sumida, B.Y., E.H. Ahlstrom, and H.G. Moser. 1979. Early development of seven flatfishes of the eastern north Pacific with heavily pigmented larvae (Pisces, Pleuronectiformes). U.S. Fish. Bull. 77(1):105-145.

Sumida, B.Y., and H.G. Moser. 1980. Food and feeding of Pacific hake larvae, *Merluccius productus*, off southern California and Baja California. CalCOFI Rep. 21:161-166.

Taning, A.V. 1918. Mediterranean Scopelidae (*Saurus, Aulopus, Chloropthalmus*, and *Myctophum*). Rep. Danish Oceanogr. Exped. 1908-10. 2(A7), 54 pp.

―――. 1923. *Lophius*. Rep. Danish Oceanogr. Exped. 1908-10, 2(A 10), 30 pp.

―――. 1955. On the breeding areas of the swordfish (*Xiphias*). Papers in Marine Biology and Oceanography. Suppl. to Vol. 3, Deep-Sea Res. 137:438-450.

―――. 1961. Larval and postlarval stages of *Sebastes* species and *Helicolenus dactylopterus*. Rap. P.-V., Reun, Cons. Perm. int. Explor. Mer 150:234-240.

Tortonese, E. 1956. Plectognathi. *In* Uova, larve e stadi giovanili di Teleostei, Fauna e Flora del Golfo di Napoli, Monogr. 38(3):960-977.

Tsukahara, H., T. Shiokawa, and T. Inao. 1957. Studies on the flying-fishes of the Amakusa Islands. Part 3. The life histories and habits of three species of the genus *Cypselurus*. Sci. Bull. Fac. Agric. Kyushu Univ. 16(2):287-302.

Uchida, K. 1936. A note on the pelagic postlarval stage of *Antigonia rubescens* (Pisces, Capriformes). The Zoological Magazine 48(11):935-939.

―――. 1958. Eggs, larvae and juvenile of *Hemiramphus sajori* (Temminck and Schlegel) (Hemirhamphidae) *In* Uchida et al., Studies on the Eggs, Larvae and Juveniles of Japanese Fishes. J. Fac. Agric. Kyushu Univ. Ser. I, 89 pp.

Voss, N.A. 1954. The postlarval development of the fishes of the family Gempylidae from the Florida Current. I. *Nesiarchus* Johnson and *Gempylus* Cuv. and Val. Bull. Mar. Sci. 4(2):120-159.

Weber, M. 1913. Die Fische der Siboga—Expedition. E.J. Brill, Leiden, 710 pp.

Weihs, D., and H.G. Moser. 1981. Stalked eyes as an adaptation towards more efficient foraging in marine fish larvae. Bull. Mar. Sci. 31(1):31-36.

Zaitsev, Yu.P. 1970. Marine Neustonology. Israel Program for Scientific Translations, Jerusalem, 207 pp.